S0-CNQ-744

THEY ANSWERED "SÍ" TO GREATNESS!

IN GOVERNMENT:

Herman Badillo—New York's fighting congressman

Joseph Montoya—the boy wonder of New Mexico politics who has become a champion of freedom and justice in the U.S. Senate

IN SPORTS:

Roberto Clemente—whose bat, glove, and personal bravery won him immortality as a player and as a man

Jim Plunkett—the star quarterback who decided to finish college before becoming a pro

IN SOCIAL SERVICE:

César Chávez—whose leadership of the California farm workers is one of the magnificent achievements of our time

IN THE ARTS:

José Limón—one of ballet's top creative geniuses

Rita Moreno—who turned her back on Hollywood rather than be racially stereotyped, and became a brilliant Broadway star

These are but a few of the vivid personalities you will meet on these pages. Here are men and women whose success is matched by their pride in their Spanish heritage. Here are superb representatives of one of America's great human resources—her Spanish-speaking people.

SIGNET and MENTOR Titles of Related Interest

RISING VOICES

Profiles of
Hispano-American
Lives

By

Al Martínez

A SIGNET BOOK

NEW AMERICAN LIBRARY

TIMES MIRROR

For my wife,
Joanne,
without whom this book
would not have
been written.

SIGNET, SIGNET CLASSICS,
MENTOR, PLUME and MERIDIAN BOOKS
are published by The New American Library, Inc.,
1301 Avenue of the Americas, New York, New York 10019

First Printing, April, 1974

2 3 4 5 6 7 8 9

PRINTED IN THE UNITED STATES OF AMERICA

Acknowledgments

The author gratefully acknowledges the assistance of Mr. J. Edward Atkinson, senior public relations supervisor, Carnation Company, for counsel and guidance from initial conception to completion of this book. Kenneth Hayes and Dixie Browne of the *Los Angeles Times* library were generous in making available the library's extensive resources. Maria Reachi's understanding of the Hispano-American culture and her research efforts were invaluable. My thanks also to these patient and thorough researchers: Lee Matthew and Maxine Greene of Carnation Company. Of course, to the subjects of these biographies who supplied information I am especially grateful. Also to Alvaro Guzmán Guzmán, I am indebted for his superlative translation of my book into Spanish.

Author's Note

Pride. The word whispers through the lives of great men. Pride in accomplishment. Pride in heritage. Pride in contribution.

Pride stands with them in adversity, fills their hours of often unbearable loneliness, enhances their creative spirit, disciplines their sciences, gives them voice in a crowd, and bends them forward, fists clenched, into the teeth of the storm.

Those whose brief biographies we present here epitomize the word at its fullest meaning.

They are special human beings. They would be special in any culture, but they stand the taller for odds they have overcome to bring Hispano-American backgrounds into high recognition in an often hostile Anglo society.

Not everyone who deserves to be is included here. The frustrating limits of word space have forced us to be arbitrary. We had to choose.

Those finally selected—artists, educators, sportsmen, labor leaders, entertainers, government workers, scientists, clergymen, communicators, jurists—represent the best of those who, with pride and style, have brought honor to their heritage and richness to our world.

Their voices rise across the land.

AL MARTÍNEZ

Los Angeles, 1973

Preface

Much of American history has been a story of individualism and self-reliance. Competition and the struggle for success encouraged us to look to ourselves first and be willing to set aside the feelings of others if need be. As a result, most of the time the losers in political life or economic competition had to get along as best they could. Racial and cultural minorities usually suffered at the hands of the American majority, forced to change their ways and adapt to the Anglo mode of life. The blacks, Indians, and the Hispano-Americans have borne a heavy burden.

It is clear today that we can no longer ignore minorities, and that we can no longer force them to pay the price for being different. We sense the need for greater understanding among all Americans. This book is a contribution toward this need.

Rising Voices has value for all ages. However, it is directed primarily at younger people. In a sense, it is directed toward the young at heart, those who have an open mind and a curiosity about culturally different people in our society. The value of the book lies in the fact that it opens a door. It is not the complete story about Hispano-Americans in the United States, but it will sharpen the appetite for learning more about this important and large group.

The idea behind the book is that we can come to know a people by knowing some of its distinguished individuals. This method is practical in light of the differences we find among Hispano-Americans. No one group of Hispano-Americans can represent all the rest. There are too many differences between Mexicans, Puerto Ricans, and Argentines, for example. They share the Spanish language (except for Brazilians, who speak Portuguese), religion, and many attitudes about life. The national differences are often pronounced, however, and these differences persist in the United States. The differences can be as long-lived and as clear as those be-

tween Englishmen and Scots, for example. Indeed, like the
Irish and the English, many Hispano-Americans have waged
war against each other. Thus the book shows good judgment
in biographizing individuals of each major Hispano-American
group in the United States.

Among the ideas that most Hispano-Americans share, we
find a common view of the hemisphere. Their view is rather
unlike ours. For most Hispano-Americans, as we call them,
America is not a country. America is a continent. The United
States is a country in America, but it is not representative of
America. Hispano-Americans all assume that they are Americans, as well as Cubans or Mexicans. It is a duality that they
are familiar with, and it poses no problems. It is pretty much
like dual citizenship in the United States, by which we are
citizens of the country and of a particular state as well. When
they come to live in the United States, Hispano-Americans
face some new problems of identity. They hear citizens of the
United States speak as if they alone are Americans, as if they
owned the word and the idea. Unlike European immigrants
to the United States, Hispano-Americans have a feeling of
continental brotherhood.

The book does not relate different Hispano-American
groups to each other; it simply tells us about some fifty-two
Hispano-Americans who have gained fame or professional
success in the society of the United States. The measure for
success is *estadounidense* ("United-Stateser"). That is, the
individuals we read about here have been picked according
to success standards in the United States. In Hispano-Latin
America, somewhat different standards might be used. Since
we are studying the Hispano-American groups in our own society, our standards are the more significant.

Our schools have tended to ignore the culture and contributions of Hispano-Americans to our society. For the most part,
when Hispano-Americans appear in textbooks, they appear
as problems and issues. This is particularly true of Mexicans
and Puerto Ricans. Like other minority groups, they have
been pressured to become "American." They have tried to
melt into the so-called melting pot. Many have succeeded in
"passing" as other Americans. Schools have tried to Amer-
icanize Hispano-Americans, but many have refused to give
up their own cultural heritage. The schools have often taught
Hispano-Americans that they are not truly American. By re-
jecting their Hispano-American culture, schools have in
effect taught the children of Hispano-Americans that there

was something wrong with them. Often their parents have suffered prejudice in jobs, housing, and social life. The overall educational achievement of Hispano-Americans has been poor, and their life has been injured by this great deficiency. Today most Hispano-Americans are intensifying their long struggle for respect and equality in the United States.

Fortunately, today we find that schools are achieving a broader, more realistic view of Hispano-Americans. Cultural differences can cause misunderstandings, but now we have concluded that the advantages of bilingual culture can far outweigh the disadvantages. The bilingual child need not be disadvantaged. If his ability is preserved and developed, he has a great advantage over the monolingual child. The same applies to cultural ingredients that Hispano-Americans preserve in our society.

As the world shrinks, as we become more interdependent for resources and economic markets, as the world becomes more polluted and more dangerous, we are reexamining cultural differences. Hispano-Americans have always been there, and many of them have lived within our borders before we became a nation in 1776. Hispano-Americans to the south of us and Hispano-Americans living among us are now recognized for what they always were—a great human and cultural resource.

DR. JULIÁN NAVA

Contents

Introduction

Children are impressionable. They learn from the examples of their parents and elders. And their young, fresh minds are molded by observation and emulation.

By such means their culture is handed down from generation to generation, through both formal and informal education. Values, life styles, religious beliefs, and inspiring examples of heroes are learned, respected, and performed by the emerging generations, who in turn pass these attributes on to their progeny.

Anglo-Americans have a cultural history depicting their indigenous heroes in studies, literature, and art forms.

There are some Americans, however, whose ethnic origins are different from their majority counterparts. They have heroes, but they are from Mexico, Cuba, Brazil, Japan, or other mother lands.

They are ethnic heroes, and they have not been recognized by most Americans as heroes of the United States.

So with what exemplars can Spanish-speaking children identify? American folklore includes few accomplished and well-known Americans of Spanish-speaking descent. Those who have achieved fame are purported bandits such as California's Joaquin Murrieta and Mexico's Pancho Villa.

A lack of examples, along with cultural barriers, has been responsible for an obstruction in excellence among Spanish-speaking youth.

But the barriers are coming down. Progress indicates the promise of vertical mobility for the Spanish-speaking, a movement out of their present class or status.

The mobility is evident in the increasing numbers of public officials, school-board trustees, college students, and highly placed federal officials. It is also evident in social, economic, and educational advancement.

Artificial barriers of discrimination based on race, color, and creed are being eliminated. The problem of discrimina-

1

tion has been challenged by the Constitution. It has made its way into executive orders from the President's office and into the courts for clarification. Huge sums are being spent to finance the elimination of discrimination.

And the barriers keep coming down. Laws, decisions, executive orders, and public funds are changing the souls, minds, and spirits of this nation. Americans are coming to a fuller sense of fair play.

The personalities of this book have encountered the barriers of prejudice and discrimination so familiar to those of the Spanish-speaking culture.

The list of exemplary Americans of Spanish-surnamed background reflected here should spark the imaginations of our young people and stimulate a "can-do" attitude. It has the potential to produce hundreds of similar Americans.

This book fills the void of desperately needed Spanish-speaking heroes. It is a landmark that provides a fertile ground for our young generation to develop its dreams into realistic opportunities.

DR. HENRY M. RAMÍREZ

Lieutenant Commander Everett Álvarez, Jr.

Lieutenant Commander Everett Álvarez, Jr.

When Lieutenant Commander Everett Álvarez, Jr., suspected that peace was coming at last to Vietnam and that he might be released after almost nine years as a Communist prisoner of war, he wrote his family, "When I come home, keep calm."

Here was a man who for 3,103 days had endured despair, loneliness, and uncertainty—a POW for longer than all but one man in American history; yet his chief concern was with those he was returning to rather than with the deprivation he had suffered.

And when finally he was brought back to the United States, his first reaction was one of gratitude, not anger at the circumstances of his confinement or sorrow at the freedom that had been taken from him.

"For years and years we've dreamed of this day," Álvarez told the crowd who greeted the POWs at a northern California airfield. "And we kept faith—faith in God, in our President, and in our country. It was this faith that maintained our hope that someday our dreams would come true, and today they have.

"You did not forget us."

Lieutenant Commander Álvarez, then a lieutenant junior grade, was shot down in his jet fighter on August 5, 1964, while attacking a PT-boat base in North Vietnam. He was only the second American taken prisoner in the long and controversial war in Southeast Asia.

Born in Salinas, California, two days before Christmas in 1937, he is a second-generation Mexican-American. His parents were laborers and farm workers.

5

Young Everett worked his way through both high school and college, where he was active in football and track. In 1960 he received a degree in electrical engineering from the University of Santa Clara, and upon graduation entered the Naval Aviation Officers Candidate Program.

Álvarez won his commission that first year, received general flight instruction, and in 1961, jet training. His first tour of duty was at Lemore Naval Air Station in central California, followed by a 1963 cruise aboard the aircraft carrier *Constellation.*

He was on a second cruise in Asian waters when he was shot down, the first American taken prisoner in North Vietnam itself. The first man captured in the war, a soldier, was taken in the South, and had been held prisoner longer than any other military man in American history.

Life in a foreign military prison was not the only sorrow in the young naval officer's life. He had been married a brief seven months before his capture. His wife waited for her husband for six years and then revealed she had "fallen out of love with him" and could wait no longer. She divorced him and remarried.

"I hope," Álvarez wrote later, "her present husband loves her as much as I did." "That shows," his ex-wife said softly, "what a wonderful person Everett is."

Álvarez was among the first group of American prisoners released by the Communists when the war ended. Twenty friends and relatives watched on television as he stepped from the Air Force jet in the Philippines. There were cries of joy and relief as the commander, thin but otherwise fit, smiled and saluted.

"I am so filled with inner happiness," his mother sobbed, "I cannot talk. I cannot express it."

Lieutenant Commander Álvarez, now thirty-five, came home to a world that had altered considerably since he had been taken from it almost a decade ago. He expressed fascination with the new automobiles, television, cassette tape recorders, women's liberation, and mini-skirts—which, he admitted modestly, he liked.

His hometown of Santa Clara near San Francisco expressed its pleasure in having their man back by turning out 100,000 strong at a parade in his honor.

Álvarez thanked them for the parade, for their letters, for the fact that they *cared,* then added a somber note. "Remember," he said, "the many prisoners who are unaccounted for, and those who will never come back."

Manuel Aragón, Jr.

Manuel Aragón, Jr.

The third-highest-ranking public administrator in the third-largest city of the United States is a young Mexican-American who believes that, in the arena of public service, if you aren't part of the solution, you're part of the problem. And Manuel Aragón, Jr., did not accept the job as deputy mayor of Los Angeles to be anyone's problem.

To the contrary, the adult history of the forty-two-year-old ex-fruit picker flashes with epochs of social involvement that have kept him seeking solutions to problems and betterment of the human condition since his undergraduate days at Berkeley.

Many predict that the concern, backed by extraordinary political acumen, may someday carry him to Sacramento as California's first Mexican-American governor.

The eldest of nine children whose records of intellectual and social achievement are not dissimilar from the Kennedys', Manuel was born in Los Angeles and raised in Arizona. The family returned to California when he was sixteen and were forced by economic circumstances to join the state's huge agricultural labor force.

Young Aragón dropped out of high school eventually and took a full-time job to help support the family. Shortly thereafter he joined the Air Force for a four-year hitch.

After his discharge, Manuel turned to education and social involvement. As a student at Los Angeles City College, he won academic honors and was elected student-body president.

Then he entered the University of California at Berkeley,

where he joined a student political party called SLATE—
considered somewhat radical in 1958 but mild by comparison
to what followed in the 1960's. SLATE protested nuclear
testing and racial discrimination.

Aragón ran for student-body president as a young radical
and lost; but he lost more than an election. Time spent on the
race cost him grades, and he was dismissed because of an in-
complete academic record.

It was a sobering experience for the youthful idealist. "I
was a candidate for Phi Beta Kappa and lost that. I wanted
to graduate from Berkeley, and I lost that."

The setback was temporary. Aragón went on to receive a
degree in economics and political science from San Francisco State, and a few years later joined the Department of
Commerce's Economic Development Administration.

Aragón rose to manager of the forty-million-dollar program
that covered federal growth projects throughout southern
California, and established himself at age thirty-five as a man
to be reckoned with in the politics of public service.

Two years later Aragón was selected over more than a hundred other candidates to become executive director of the
Economic and Youth Opportunities Agency of Los Angeles.

As chief executive officer of a three-hundred-man organization with an annual budget of fifty million dollars, Aragón
headed one of the nation's largest antipoverty programs for
a year.

He resigned and became president of the City of Commerce
Investment Company, specializing in loans to minority-owned
businesses, and later became producer-host of the highly
regarded television show *Impacto*, a public affairs program
concentrating on the plight of the Mexican-American.

The other six brothers in the remarkable family, meanwhile, weren't sitting still: Robert, with an M.A. from Harvard, became director of the Los Angeles Urban Coalition;
Charles established his own business; Joseph, a graduate of
USC Law School, is with the American Bar Association;
George is studying for his Ph.D. at Harvard; Conrad pursues
a Ph.D. at Yale; and Luis has just graduated from Yale.

The two sisters, Alicia and Rachel, are married and raising
their own families.

All of the brothers have been active in politics, and when
Tom Bradley, the first black mayor in the history of Los
Angeles, was swept into office in 1973, he picked Manuel as
one of his two deputies.

Aragón's selection was well received. Bradley has made it clear that the bright, pragmatic Mexican-American was never intended to be the administration's "token Mexican," and chicano activists believe that their new representation in the affairs of city government is far more than just ceremonial.

Aragón himself, despite strong cultural ties, feels that he owes the Mexican-American community no more and no less than what he owes all the people of the big city: "a promise to do the best job as cleanly and honestly as I can." It's an idea Aragón has been expounding for years. It's called being part of the solution.

Martina Arroyo

Martina Arroyo

Martina Arroyo's father used to tell her to "keep stepping ahead." It was advice not wasted on the dreamy and impressionable young girl, for in subsequent years she would discover a magnificent talent within herself and would step ahead to build that talent into what many came to regard as among the world's most beautiful singing voices. Martina Arroyo, "the reigning queen of Verdi opera," became an international prima donna with few equals.

Born and raised in the black ghetto of Harlem, Martina's father was a native of Spain and had come to New York via Puerto Rico. Her mother was from South Carolina. Martina, her parents, and her older brother were a close-knit family.

Although she received little formal musical training as a child, Martina was taught piano and often sang in the church choir. She took ballet lessons for years.

Possibly more important to her future career, her parents made it a point to show their children the world outside of the ghetto. Rarely a weekend passed without a movie, a play, a stage show, a circus, a rodeo, or a dance recital beyond the harsh boundaries of Harlem.

Miss Arroyo remembers now that a movie may have first piqued her interest in music. "I think that's where the idea of singing opera first hit me. In one or another of those pictures Dorothy Kirsten sang 'Un Bel Di,' and I began dreaming of being 'Madame Butterball.'"

It was in Hunter High School that the young girl who was to become one of the world's great divas was first noticed as a singer. The director of an opera workshop heard her sing and called a voice teacher to say, "I have a very strange case here, a girl I consider the greatest future talent. She knows nothing about opera and wants to be a teacher. Would you do me the favor of listening to her?"

The teacher would indeed, and Martina Arroyo's formal lessons began. She still studies with Mrs. Marinka Gurewich.

She sang as she went through college, and after one recital a concert manager offered to work for her for a minimum fee "until you can afford me." Miss Arroyo accepted. She remains with the Displicer agency.

Upon her graduation from college in three years, she worked for a while as a schoolteacher and then as a social worker, but they were only part of the "stepping ahead" her father had told her to do. In 1958 she competed in the New York Metropolitan Opera Company's Auditions of the Air and won one thousand dollars.

That same year Miss Arroyo performed in the American premiere of Pizzetti's opera *Murder in the Cathedral.* And shortly after that she sang at the Met as the offstage celestial voice in *Don Carlo.*

She pursued fame throughout Europe, where many young artists receive their start, and soon was toasted as one of the continent's best lyrico-spinto sopranos. And then, in February 1965, with less than two days' notice, Martina Arroyo was invited back to the Met to substitute for Birgit Nilsson in the title role of *Aïda.*

Her performance won rave notices, and she was immediately offered a star contract for leading roles in *Il Trovatore, Don Carlo, Madame Butterfly,* and again *Aïda.* Miss Arroyo has appeared at the Met in every subsequent season, and in 1968 made opera history by singing the part of Elsa in Wagner's *Lohengrin,* a role traditionally reserved for blond women of Germanic appearance.

Miss Arroyo became greatly in demand in London, Paris, Rome, Buenos Aires, Tel Aviv, and Vienna, and in opera houses from San Francisco to Boston. A friend remarked that she is so sought after that one could almost schedule a round-the-world trip and hear Martina sing in operas, concerts, and recitals all along the way.

She has also appeared on American, British, and German television, the latter of which devoted a special to her talent called *The Beautiful Voice.* And in between times she has produced records for Decca, Angel, Philips, London, RCA, and Columbia.

Each year, Martina makes sixty to seventy opera appearances, and critics believe her voice is still growing, still maturing. That pleases the great international prima donna. For didn't her father tell her those many years ago to keep stepping ahead?

Bishop Juan Arzube

Bishop Juan Arzube

In an era that measures men by the extent of their involvement, Bishop Juan Arzube stands exceedingly tall. He is a man in touch with his time, a vocal participant in the issues of the day. As the *Los Angeles Times* remarked, the prelate "has shown few signs of performing quietly in the background."

There is reason for the observation. Not too long after he was ordained as one of three auxiliary Catholic bishops in Los Angeles, the Most Reverend Bishop Arzube officiated at a Mass for jet hijacker Ricardo Chávez-Ortiz and his family. There was criticism.

"I have been asked," said Bishop Arzube, "why I am offering such a Mass. I answer: Why shouldn't I? Chávez-Ortiz needs help from God, his family needs help, and the Mexican people for whom he did it [the hijacking] also need help."

The response is typical of the man. He does what he feels must be done, public criticism notwithstanding, and is not afraid to engage in some "sermonizing" when the need arises. Into an invocation at a Los Angeles Press Club banquet once he inserted the prayer that reporters concentrate less on sensational and disturbing news.

Bishop Arzube, the first native Ecuadorian ever to serve in the United States Catholic hierarchy, was born in the picturesque seaside city of Guayaquil in 1918. No child of poverty, his father was one of Ecuador's most respected gynecologists and was anxious that Juan and his two sisters should receive the best education.

The boy began his education at the Christian Brothers School in Guayaquil; then, at the age of nine, he was taken to Great Britain for his schooling. He came back home in

17

1932, where he received his Bachelor of Arts degree in philosophy from the Colegio Vicente Rocafuerte in Guayaquil.

Juan had meanwhile decided that engineering was to be his field of endeavor, and went on to enroll as a graduate student at Rensselaer Polytechnic Institute in Troy, New York. Four years later he had his degree in civil engineering.

His first job, as a specialist in health and sanitation, was supervision of the construction of a hospital for children's ailments and disorders. But even that demanding a vocation wasn't enough for the active Juan Arzube. He returned to New York for more study to expand his knowledge in engineering.

But while in New York, he decided to move to Los Angeles, where new opportunities beckoned. He went to work at a correspondence school monitoring English lessons and translating them into his native tongue. And in Los Angeles, he studied radio techniques and developed his talents into a lead role for the CBS series *Romance of the Ranchos*. But even all of this still wasn't enough.

Then, a retreat he made at Malibu along the foamy Pacific coast changed his life in 1945. While reciting the Lord's Prayer, Arzube suddenly seized upon the phrase "Thy will be done" and realized for the first time that he really meant it. The realization is what theologians describe as "an experimental knowledge of God."

He enrolled at St. John's Seminary in 1948 as a divinity student for the Archdiocese of Los Angeles and was ordained into the priesthood six years later.

Father Arzube held many posts in downtown Los Angeles, East Los Angeles, and the south-central part of the city. In addition to serving the Holy Name Society at the archdiocesan level, he supervised erection of the handsome shrine of Our Lady of Guadalupe, a mission church of which he was named canonical administrator.

Then in 1968 Father Arzube was elevated to the episcopacy as titular bishop of Civitate and auxiliary to the metropolitan archbishop of Los Angeles. He was ordained in 1971.

Still active, still involved, Bishop Arzube has proved time and again that he is not afraid to confront, and that he is able to do so with skill and wit.

He illustrated his capacity for both at a banquet once when a comic made reference to Pope Paul's birth-control encyclical by saying, "Those who don't play the game shouldn't make the rules."

At the end of the gathering, just before delivering the benediction, Bishop Arzube, referring to the comic's statement,
observed, "I don't lay eggs, but I can cook them better than
any chicken." Then he gave the benediction.

Congressman Herman Badillo

Congressman Herman Badillo

An astute political veteran once observed that Herman Badillo has "that certain something." It slices through emotional confusion, deadening bureaucratic response, and useless ceremonial ritual to confront the needs of the people he represents in Congress, and it has made him an increasingly significant power in United States government. Not bad for an orphan boy from East Harlem.

The first native Puerto Rican ever elected as a voting member of the House of Representatives, Badillo was born in Caguas, Puerto Rico, in 1929. His father died in a tuberculosis epidemic when Herman was five, and his mother four years later of the same disease. Both were tragically young.

Their son went to live with relatives. At the age of eleven, he came to the United States and finally settled in New York, where he attended public school. It was in school that Badillo began to emerge.

A brilliant student, he supported himself through college by washing dishes, working as a short-order cook, and setting up pins in a bowling alley. In 1951 he graduated *magna cum laude* from the City College of New York with a Bachelor of Business Administration degree.

Badillo went to work immediately as a full-time accountant, simultaneously studying law at night, and in 1954 he was graduated *cum laude* from Brooklyn Law School—where he was on the *Law Review,* won the first scholarship prize of the graduating class, and was class valedictorian.

Intelligent and hard-working, two characteristics he had already proved beyond doubt, Badillo's "certain something" began to emerge in 1960 when he entered politics by setting up the John F. Kennedy Democratic Club in East Harlem.

The following year he challenged a party regular for the post of district leader in the Sixteenth Assembly District and lost by only seventy-five votes.

Badillo was demanding a recount when Mayor Robert Wagner appointed him deputy real-estate commissioner, and then, in 1962, commissioner of the Department of Relocation. It was the highest appointive office ever held by a Puerto Rican in New York.

Seven years later he decided it was time to try for the big one, the job of Mayor of New York City. He entered the Democratic primary in 1969 and ran a strong third in a field of five candidates. It was a remarkable showing for someone so new in citywide politics, but he wasn't satisfied.

The following year Badillo ran for Congress in New York's new twenty-first district — and won with a stunning eighty-five percent of the vote. He was not only the first person of Puerto Rican birth ever to be a voting member of the House, but he was also the highest officeholder of Puerto Rican extraction in the United States.

He plunged into the rough world of federal politics as though he had been born to it. When he was appointed to the Agriculture Committee, he challenged the assignment before the House Democratic caucus.

Badillo felt he deserved more than that, and so did *The New York Times,* which called that first appointment "an insulting waste of Badillo's talents." The caucus relented, and he was named to the important Education and Labor Committee, which handles most antipoverty legislation.

His first speech on the House floor called for the government to lend twenty billion dollars to America's cities until a federal revenue-sharing program was enacted. He has also led efforts to expand the bilingual education programs, to end the nuisance of jet noise, and to get Puerto Rico its fair share of federal funds.

And he helped break a deadlock over the 1.5-billion-dollar Nixon administration school-desegregation bill — after an addition to the measure was written in setting aside four percent for bilingual education.

Badillo, who makes himself readily available to his constituents, has organized a council in his diverse district composed of all the district's interests to keep him informed of the needs of the people he represents.

He simultaneously welcomes advice but is a man who makes his own decisions. Wrote an author for *New York Magazine*: "Badillo thinks he doesn't need anybody. It isn't arrogance. It is rather a belief in his destiny."

U.S. Treasurer Romana Bañuelos

U.S. Treasurer Romana Bañuelos

When Romana Bañuelos arrived in Los Angeles from Mexico in 1944, she had thirty-six cents in her pocket and a fierce pride in her heart. The money represented the last of the savings she was gambling on a new life. The pride was based on a deep conviction that to be a Mexican was to be something special.

In the years that followed, the willingness to gamble and the pride in her ancestry translated themselves into a remarkable success story for a woman whom adversity could not master. She became treasurer of the United States and founder of a wholesale food concern that does a five million-dollar-a-year business.

Mrs. Bañuelos was born in the small mining town of Miami, Arizona, in 1925. Seven years later, the depression cost her father his job, and they were advised to return to Mexico, where both parents had been born.

As a result, young Romana was raised in the state of Sonora as a Mexican and eagerly absorbed the stories of the men who built pyramids in Mexico in the centuries when the rest of the American continent was a wilderness.

Married at sixteen, she and her husband moved to El Paso, Texas. Two years and two sons later, they were divorced. Life was hard for a while. She worked in a laundry for a dollar a day to survive, but Romana Bañuelos abandoned neither her pride nor a dream that there were better things ahead.

In pursuit of the dream, she went to Los Angeles, took a job washing dishes, and saved money. When she had saved four hundred dollars, an aunt borrowed money to join her as a partner, and they bought a small tortilla factory.

Mrs. Bañuelos recalls: "I used to get up at two in the morning and grind the corn and make the tortillas and pack them. Then I would go home and cook breakfast for the children and make their lunches and get them off to school. Then I would go back to the factory and cook the corn to be ready to grind the next day."

On the first day of business, she and her aunt made a total of $36. That has since grown to $23,000 a day.

She remarried, and her husband worked at another job to help keep the factory going in the difficult early days, but eventually the entire family—including a daughter now—pitched in at the plant to make it a success. Today there are three hundred employees.

But Mrs. Bañuelos didn't stop there. Acutely aware of the needs of her Mexican-American community, she was instrumental in establishing the Pan American National Bank of East Los Angeles in 1964.

"It was the same old story at first. They said we didn't have qualified businessmen. That's the usual excuse to stop people of Mexican descent from doing something. They say, 'You're not qualified, you can't make it.'"

But they did make it. The bank was opened in a small trailer, and those concerned—including Romana Bañuelos—began selling stock to the community. From a hesitant beginning, it has grown to an institution with resources of twenty-two million dollars.

Mrs. Bañuelos' business acumen, determination, and pride in her ethnic origin did not go unnoticed in a nation abruptly aware of the inequities suffered by its citizens with Spanish names. In 1971 President Nixon appointed her treasurer of the United States. She became the first Mexican-American woman to be named to such a high post.

Of her success, Mrs. Bañuelos says, "The best thing that ever happened to me was that my mother and father left the United States when I was young, and I was raised without prejudice in Mexico.

"Nobody can tell me that it is bad to be of Mexican descent. Nobody can convince me that a Mexican cannot be successful. You must know the story of your culture and be proud of your ancestors."

Mrs. Bañuelos believes that the greatest need for Mexican youngsters living in this country is a good education. Toward that end, she has established a scholarship foundation to help the children of the barrios. Three of those on scholarships entered UCLA. Mrs. Bañuelos is determined to see that number increase.

Amalia Betanzos

Amalia Betanzos

Amalia Victoria Betanzos often wondered as she worked toward a university degree how she would someday use her education to help improve the quality of life for her fellow Puerto Ricans. A child of the South Bronx, she knew better than most the conditions that existed for many of her people in New York. What worried her was that she might never be able to improve those conditions. Her concern was real. She would prove that.

Mrs. Betanzos—whose efforts eventually embraced the needs of all racial minorities—went out from New York University with a Bachelor of Arts degree, determined to help those who could not help themselves.

Her birth in the South Bronx to a Puerto Rican mother and a Spanish father had given her a special feeling for the area's people and their problems. When much later she was named commissioner of New York City's Youth Services Agency, Mrs. Betanzos would say, "I know the meaning of poverty, what it means to give those kids better housing and a better education. I know the meaning of prejudice."

After NYU, the ambitious young woman involved herself with local antipoverty groups and the Federal Head Start program. Her ability and sincerity were quickly noticed, and in 1968 Mrs. Betanzos was named executive director of the nation's largest Puerto Rican antipoverty agency, the Puerto Rican Community Development Project.

It was her first major post, directing programs to obtain jobs for the unemployed and organizing blocks to participate in legal and drug-treatment services.

Two years later she joined Mayor Lindsay's staff as an assistant, and soon became the first woman to hold the position of executive secretary to the mayor. He later appointed her a member of the City Commission on Human Rights.

Mrs. Betanzos also served as New York's commissioner of relocation, a position that suited her emotionally as well as professionally. Her belief that all Americans had a right to adequate housing had often expressed itself in nonofficial situations.

A friend recalls, for instance, "the many occasions when Amy [her nickname] would prevent evictions of poor families by defying authorities and standing in front of the doorways until a relocation was made and funds obtained to take care of the people."

Another friend remembers her work on behalf of those whose homes were lost in fires, her efforts to find them new apartments near their place of employment.

Mrs. Betanzos' work benefited those in need, and her reputation grew. A Democrat who had actively campaigned for Mayor Lindsay, she once served as citywide coordinator of Puerto Ricans for Lindsay. Nevertheless, her work was praised by conservatives as well as liberals, and when in 1972 she was named to head the important New York City Youth Services Agency, the appointment was almost universally acknowledged to be a good one.

It was the kind of job Mrs. Betanzos, with a husband and son of her own, was meant for. She went at it with customary enthusiasm and found there was much to do. "And all through those years of education," she would say with a shake of the head, "I worried about what I could accomplish for the young, the old, and the underprivileged."

Mayor Lindsay has called New York's resourceful Amy "a distinguished public servant who combines compassion, shrewdness, and a capacity for hard nuts-and-bolts work in difficult assignments."

Mrs. Betanzos shrugs. Standing on a reviewing platform as young marchers in a Columbus Day parade streamed by her up Manhattan's Fifth Avenue, she waved at them and said, "Our minority kids—blacks, Puerto Ricans, whatever the grouping—are our future, and they are my concern."

Then, with a smile that more than emphasized her point, she added, "Look at those youngsters—aren't they beautiful?"

Dr. Francisco Bravo

Dr. Francisco Bravo

Ask Dr. Francisco Bravo how he spends his time, and he could reply as a surgeon, pharmacist, medical administrator, agriculturist, cattle rancher, banker, and civic worker. For these are among the occupations and avocations he has pursued with equal enthusiasm over the years, and while they have made him a lot of money they have also brought him a great deal of satisfaction.

A man of enormous energy, Dr. Bravo has also learned to measure his vitality into a variety of altruistic activities that include the Bravo Scholarship Foundation for Mexican-Americans, the Medical Program for Mexican Braceros in the United States, the Youth Opportunity Foundation, and the Governor's Committee on Employment of the Handicapped.

And even that is still only a small part of his full schedule. The lives of concerned men brim over with action.

Born in California's Ventura County in 1910 of Mexican parents, young Francisco worked hard at manual labor in the fields around Santa Paula to earn extra money for himself and his family. It was not a negative experience. He gained great love for farms and farm animals.

After graduation from Santa Paula High School, Bravo began applying his energy to academic pursuits. And before he was through with his studies at the University of Southern California and Stanford, he had his bachelor's degree, his master's degree in sociology, and his medical degree. On top of that he threw in four additional years of specialty training in surgery, became a pharmaceutical chemist, and was made a fellow of the American College of Abdominal Surgeons.

But even that was only a beginning. Dr. Bravo, stimulated

by his youthful interest, bought a thirteen-acre ranch where he and his wife began raising cattle. The Second World War, in which he served as an Army surgeon in the South and Central Pacific, interrupted that effort, but after the war Dr. Bravo returned to his multiplicity of activities.

As he was founding the Bravo Clinic in Los Angeles, for instance, he was also buying more land to raise more cattle, pigs, and purebred Arabian horses, relying heavily on his boyhood experience and nearby experts to assist him in the beginning. Eventually the Bravos expanded their activities to include growing barley, alfalfa, hay, grain, and sugar beets.

In addition to his full-time medical concerns, Dr. Bravo became president of the Southern California Hereford Association, a committeeman for the Great Western Livestock Show of Los Angeles, vice-chairman of the Los Angeles Chamber of Commerce Agricultural Committee, a member of the University of California Advisory Agriculture Council, and a member of the State Board of Agriculture.

Not that it all happened overnight. Even for a man of Dr. Bravo's enormous enthusiasm for ranching, carrying on a heavy medical practice in the East Los Angeles barrio precluded spending all the time he would like at what had become three ranches.

But when he was at the ranch, he was more than the gentleman farmer simply directing a busy staff. He became personally involved. Wrote a newspaper agricultural columnist: "Dr. Bravo dug wells, fought hardpan soil to create pastures, and created the cleanest piggery in the world."

Spreading one's time between ranching and medicine— each in itself a demanding undertaking—would have taxed the resources of even the most remarkable of men, but not Francisco Bravo. He became medical examiner for the California State Athletic Commission, commissioner of health for Los Angeles, president of the city's Board of Police Commissioners, a member of a Blue Ribbon Committee to Revise the City Charter, a member of the board of the Los Angeles County Mental Health Association, and a member of the National Conference on Christians and Jews.

And in between times he founded and became president of the Pan American National Bank of East Los Angeles.

Dr. Bravo has received many honors over his long and distinguished career, but one that pleased him most honored his work for the past quarter of a century in encouraging children interested in agriculture, medicine, and business.

Dr. Edgar Buttari

Vikki Carr

When Vikki Carr sings, her lovely voice silences a noisy night-club audience. When Florencia Bisenta de Casillas Martínez Cardona speaks, people listen. The ability to command attention with the beauty of music and the qualities of ideas are important to Vikki and Florencia, because to be gifted is not in itself enough. One must be talented *and* involved. Vikki and Florencia are both. They're the same person.

Born Florencia Bisenta de Casillas Martínez Cardona in El Paso, Texas, Miss Carr is one of the world's leading female pop singers and the only one of Mexican-American heritage who has climbed to the top as a major recording and night-club star.

She was the eldest of seven children and recalls the hard times of her childhood. The family was poor. "Many times our milk was flour and water, the meal was cactus."

They moved to southern California in Florencia's infancy, and she made her musical debut at age four, singing "Adeste Fidelis" in Latin in a Christmas program.

In high school she signed up for all the music courses she could get, and participated in musical productions. On weekends she sang with local bands until graduation, when she was offered the job of soloist with Pepe Callahan's Mexican-Irish Band.

From there it was on to international stardom.

Miss Carr was not always as fiercely proud of her heritage as she is now. "When I began school, Spanish was my first language, and I was punished for not speaking English. I wasn't as dark as many of the other Mexican kids, and they used to say I was Spanish."

Then her father, Carlos Cardona, took her aside and told her she was not Spanish, she was Mexican. He added, "Be what you are, and be proud of it."

Miss Carr says today, "When you're young and someone tells you what you are and shows you how to be proud, you've got a head start."

She bristles at the accusation, however subtle, that she changed her name out of shame. It was simply a question of convenience, she insists. "I have always sung Mexican songs, and I always tell audiences who I really am. There has never been any doubt about it when I'm performing."

The beautiful diminutive singer, as if to underscore her pride, has involved herself in Mexican-American Affairs. She helped raise more than fifty thousand dollars to save a Catholic high school in a poor barrio near San Antonio, Texas. And she has headlined a benefit for the Mexican-American organization Nosotros at the Hollywood Bowl.

In 1971 Miss Carr began what was to be an annual scholarship award of $1,000 for an outstanding Mexican-American youngster to attend college. But instead of one youngster, she selected eight the first year and gave a total of $5,000. Then in 1972 she selected nineteen and awarded them $11,750. In 1973, nineteen more students were awarded $11,000.

For this, and for her work on behalf of the Office of Economic Opportunity, the March of Dimes, VISTA, and the Tuberculosis Association, Vikki Carr was named Woman of the Year by the *Los Angeles Times*.

Despite an almost solid schedule of bookings—from the Persian Room in New York to a command performance before the Queen of England—Miss Carr still manages the time to sing to raise money for Mexican-American causes in out-of-the-way communities.

A recording star, she once had two albums and two singles among the nation's top one hundred records—simultaneously.

A television star, she has appeared on virtually every major network variety show and has taped half a dozen television specials in London and Mexico City, as well as in the United States.

She has performed before the President of the United States and starred in concerts around the world from Holland to Australia.

But despite the international fame of Vikki Carr, she makes it a point to remember that she is Florencia Bisenta de Casillas Martínez Cardona.

César Chávez

César Chávez

Few men, ethnic origin notwithstanding, have towered over the U.S. labor and civil-rights scene as prominently as César Chávez. Deified and vilified, his name became synonymous with the drive of the Mexican-American for social and economic equality, and he led the vast movement to lift his fellow migratory farm workers out of their long peonage. The late Robert F. Kennedy called him "one of the heroic figures of our time."

Chávez is primarily responsible for the existence of the United Farm Workers Union, AFL-CIO—the first effective agricultural union in the United States. His nationwide boycott of California table grapes, his fasts, and his long marches through the Golden State set a new style in nonviolent celebration of a cause and the realization of a dream. They were a long time coming.

César Estrada Chávez was born in Yuma, Arizona, in 1927. His father's dust-bowl farm failed in the depression of the 1930's, and the family joined other migrant farm workers. In the inequities of their existence, César's future was born.

He remembers working seven days a week and having the man who hired him disappear with his pay. He remembers searching for wild mustard greens to keep from starving, selling cigarette tinfoil to junk dealers to buy a sweater, being thrown out of Anglo sections in movie houses, walking barefoot through the mud to school, and never being able to go beyond the seventh grade.

The memories stayed with Chávez as he went off to the Navy, and afterward when he returned to farm work, this

time near Delano, California. In 1952 he was brought into the
Community Service Organization by Fred Ross, an organizer
for so-called "professional radical" Saul Alinsky, and helped
Mexican-Americans in their problems with immigration
authorities, police, and welfare boards.

During the following decade Chávez developed the techniques and the philosophy that would later make him a figure
of national importance. In 1962 he left the CSO, withdrew
his savings of twelve hundred dollars, and organized the National Farm Workers Association. *La Causa* had begun.

In the next six months he traveled through central California and talked to more than fifty-thousand farm workers,
and in the next two years the membership of his NFWA had
grown from one to seventeen hundred families. The organization by then had become strong enough to win pay raises on
two occasions, but there was still work to be done.

That same year—1965—eight-hundred migrant Filipino
grape pickers who belonged to the Agricultural Workers
Organizing Committee, AFL-CIO, went on strike. Chávez's
NFWA joined in.

The strike lasted five years, during which the two organiza-
tions merged to become the present United Farm Workers
Union, AFL-CIO. Nonviolence was the theme of *la huelga*, for
Chávez modeled his movement after the late Martin Luther
King, Gandhi, Nehru, and leaders of the peace movements.
He fasted for twenty-five days, led a three-hundred-mile hike
joined by ten-thousand sympathizers, and finally initiated the
nationwide boycott of California table grapes.

Eleven major wine-grape growers signed contracts with th[e]
UFWU early in the struggle, but the table-grape growers refused to yield. By August 1968, the year the boycott began, it
had cost the industry twenty percent of its national market.
Chávez was taking on the entire industry and, in his words,
"making the grape itself a label."

Contributions, support, and recognition of their fight were
the immense results of the incredibly successful boycott, and
the growers finally gave in. By the middle of 1970, contracts
had been signed by growers of eighty-four percent of the
nation's table grapes. The wages of farm workers went from
$1.10 to $2.10 an hour. The fight goes on.

Chávez saw the history-making victory only as "the end of
the beginning" and led his union into the vegetable-growing
industry of California's Salinas Valley. "The fight is never
about grapes or lettuce," he said. "It is always about people."

Chávez dreams about other work, in the fields of health and education, but first the man often referred to as "the Messiah of the Mexican-American civil-rights movement" feels that as long as economic inequities exist for them, "the dreams will have to wait."

Roberto Clemente

Roberto Clemente

Roberto Clemente, often described as the most skilled base-ball player the game ever produced, lived with pain and with the demanding necessity to be Roberto Clemente. A restless, highly charged man, his achievements tower over those of most athletes, but the prices one must pay for championship are often due with anguish. And Clemente paid them in full.

He drove himself with great intensity, haunted by the notion that on a given day he might have done less than he should have, thereby failing to give the fans what they deserved.

Even though plagued with constant pain from a 1954 back injury suffered in an automobile accident, Clemente tolerated no less than brilliance in his own performance; and long, sleepless nights of worrying over a bad throw were a burden few knew about.

Roberto Walker Clemente was born in Carolina, Puerto Rico, and when he was seventeen a scout for an island base-ball team saw him playing softball and offered him a contract. His ability as a player was obvious from the start. In his third year with the team—a year he batted .356—the Brooklyn Dodgers signed him for a ten-thousand-dollar bonus, the highest they had ever paid for a Latin-American player.

It was Clemente's first shot at the majors, but the Dodgers used him badly, and the following year, 1954, he joined the Pittsburgh Pirates. With the Pirates, his career began in earnest.

For the first five years with the team his batting average went past .300 only once, but his cannonball throw from right field was already becoming a hallmark of his greatness.

Then, in 1960 his bat caught fire. Roberto hit .314, blasted sixteen home runs, drove in ninety-four runs, and in the World Series against the New York Yankees, batted .310.

From then on, his batting average never dropped below .312 in a full season. His highest was .357, for a career average of .314.

One of Clemente's biggest years was 1966. He hit twenty-nine homers, thirty-one doubles, and eleven triples, and batted in 119 runs. He was voted baseball's Most Valuable Player.

By then, the reputation of Roberto Clemente had been well established. *Sport* magazine called him "a one-man team, the most amazing athlete of all time," and quoted the manager of an opposition team as saying, "He's not only the best today, he's one of the best that's ever played baseball."

The Pirates won the world championship in 1971, and it was during the World Series that year against the Baltimore Orioles that Clemente dazzled the baseball world. It wasn't so much the .414 average, the twelve hits, and the two homers, though they counted too. It was his fielding and base-running that left the crowds breathless—the impossible catches, the cannonball throws.

But excellence takes its toll. In addition to the back injuries, Clemente also suffered shoulder injuries, elbow bone chips, a serious blood clot in the leg, a pulled Achilles tendon, and even malaria and tonsilitis.

The burden of physical ailments was heavy, but the emotional load was even greater. A sensitive man, Roberto agonized over any criticism, however slight, and exhausted himself with the strain of pressure he imposed upon himself.

"No one drove himself like Clemente," says a psychiatrist who worked with the Pirates one season. "I have never seen a more intense person."

Insomnia was one of the results of his tension, and Roberto often admitted he did not sleep for nights on end. But the fans always forgave him his rare mistakes, and Clemente reciprocated by offering the best he could give at the time.

"If I don't take care of myself, if I have a bad season, I'm stealing people's money," he once said. "My conscience would not permit that."

Roberto Clemente died as he lived—giving. On December 31, 1972, he was aboard a plane loaded with relief supplies for victims of a devastating Nicaragua earthquake when the aircraft crashed at sea.

He was voted into Baseball's Hall of Fame the following year. A baseball official said quietly, "The game will never be the same—not ever again."

Plácido Domingo

Plácido Domingo

"God must have been in excellent spirits the day he created Plácido Domingo," a distinguished colleague has said. "He has everything needed for one of the greatest careers ever seen: an incredibly beautiful voice, great intelligence, unbelievable musicality, acting ability, wonderful looks, and a great heart."

The description has been repeated many ways by many people over many years. Plácido Domingo, still a rising star in one of the most accelerated operatic careers of the twentieth century, has already been hailed as one of the most exciting singers of our age, and, at thirty-two, the brilliant tenor has many years left to sing.

Born into a musical family in Madrid, Spain, in 1941, Plácido Domingo (the name means "peaceful Sunday") came by his love for music easily. His parents performed in Spanish operas throughout Spain and Latin America, and when their son was eight they settled in Mexico.

Plácido began his own career playing the piano, though there were athletic interludes in high school when he concentrated more on soccer than music, and even tried his hand at amateur bullfighting.

That out of his system, he studied at the National Conservatory of Music in Mexico City and made his first stage appearance as a baritone in a musical comedy. A former Chilean opera singer heard the boy and advised him to become a tenor. It was a suggestion that would change young Plácido's destiny.

At nineteen he sang the minor role of Borsa in *Rigoletto*,

but he considers the start of his career to be 1961, a year later, when he made his official operatic debut as Alfredo in *La Traviata* in Monterrey, Mexico.

The debut was an important milestone of an already fast-rising career, followed by invitations to perform with the Dallas Civic Opera and then in Fort Worth.

Next he heard that the Israel National Opera Company needed a tenor. Domingo sensed an opportunity to enlarge his repertory and went to Tel Aviv. He spent two and a half years in Israel, singing 280 performances in eleven roles, and the Israelis flocked to hear him.

Back in the United States in 1965, Domingo successfully auditioned for the New York City Opera and was assigned first to the roles of Don José in *Carmen* and Pinkerton in *Madame Butterfly*. Scant attention was paid the tenor initially, but the outpouring was soon to come.

The major New York critics would soon acclaim him in the title role of Don Rodrigo in the North American premiere of an ultramodern opera composed by Alberto Ginastera of Argentina.

The praise began timidly at first ("A splendid impression," wrote one), but then, as the quality of Plácido Domingo's voice became more apparent, as the number of his roles and his performances expanded here and abroad, the praise became lavish. "A phenomenon among tenors," cheered the New York *Post.* "Star quality."

Domingo's official debut at the Metropolitan Opera Company was scheduled for October 2, 1968, as Maurizio in *Adriana Lecouvreur,* a role he had sung only once befo. But just thirty-five minutes before curtain time several days earlier, Franco Corelli, who was to sing Maurizio that evening, canceled his performance, and Domingo took the role four days earlier than planned.

The murmur of critical praise rose now to a roar of acclaim. "Gifted with one of the most beautiful voices to be heard anywhere today," wrote one unabashedly. "Domingo," said another, "is almost too good to be true."

After that, his fame spread worldwide through performances in Hamburg, Berlin, Vienna, Milan, London, and Barcelona. Record albums were made, and began selling with remarkable success. Domingo's salary rose to $300,000 a year.

Often he has been accused of singing too much, and experts worry that the strain will wear hard on his voice. The big tenor—six-feet-two, 225 pounds—smiles. "The more I sing, the better I sound." Then he adds more seriously, "I cannot keep anything for tomorrow. I give it all tonight."

José Feliciano

José Feliciano

In the beginning, there was music. José Feliciano heard it in the darkness of his infancy, in a chilly Puerto Rican flat and on the streets of Spanish Harlem. He translated the sounds of the world into first the beats of its rhythm, tapping them out on the bottom of a cracker can. Then, at an age when most preschoolers are smashing their toys, he was interpreting the sounds he heard on a secondhand accordion. And then came the guitar.

Today the name Feliciano means music by a measure that few artists achieve. His mastery of it ranges from classical to blues to rock, and his acclaim is international. He has played to audiences of up to one hundred thousand. His records have sold almost one hundred million copies, and he has won two Grammy awards.

But Feliciano remains essentially an interpreter of the sounds of the world, applying style and genius to light the darkness as only a blind man can, and in a way that provides vision in a sense beyond sight.

Born blind in Lares, Puerto Rico, in 1945, young José quickly overcame the darkness. First there was the cracker can, then the accordion, then, at age nine, as his genius blossomed, the guitar—following tunes on scratchy records his mother bought.

"I couldn't go out and play and be an ordinary kid," he remembers. "So as a release, I turned to music. I think maybe fate does this to you just to see how you can survive. I survived. I had music for breakfast, lunch, and dinner."

The family moved to New York's Spanish Harlem, and before José was twelve he was playing his guitar to standing ovations in the Bronx. He sang along with it, imitating the pop singers of the day, then developing his own style. By age sixteen he was performing in the coffee houses of Greenwich Village—sometimes for coins dropped in a basket, sometimes "just for the hell of it."

Feliciano dropped out of high school just before graduation, drifted from friend to friend, developed his music, and tried not to let blindness rule his life. It was a time of maturing, of searching. Good things happened.

In 1962 he became a featured regular at the Cafe Id, where he met Janna, a young college student who would become his wife. In 1964 a talent scout "discovered" him and arranged for a recording contract with RCA. Feliciano's first single, "Everybody Do the Click," was released that year. There was a stirring of recognition. The next effort was an album, *The Voice and Guitar of José Feliciano.* He was on his way.

Feliciano sang in both English and Spanish, and his style developed a rock base with a semi-Latin beat that was unquestionably his own.

There were triumphant tours through Central and South America, where at a resort near Buenos Aires he sang to one hundred thousand screaming, shouting fans at the Mar del Plata Festival. Back in the United States, his first big hits followed: "Light My Fire," "California Dreamin'" and his first million-seller album, *Feliciano!* The name by now was magic.

"As a kid," he says today, "I knew there must have been some reason in that made me want to learn to play guitar. I was meant to live with music. I was a very persistent guy. I had many doors slammed in my face, but I have always followed the purpose of my life. I always did what I had to do."

Doing that has brought him fame that others only dream of. Feliciano has been featured on his own television special, has appeared with the top stars of TV, and has performed to sellout crowds throughout the United States, England, France, Australia, New Zealand, Japan, and many other countries.

His weekly *Feliciano,* a taped half-hour show, is syndicated to Spanish-language television stations across the United States and throughout Latin America, a measure of the artist's intense pride in his Puerto Rican heritage.

Feliciano's philosophy is altruistic: "I love people. I like to be nice to people, to give them music. I want to communicate with everyone."

José Ferrer

José Ferrer

To say that producer-director-actor-musician José Ferrer is talented and versatile would be to repeat, in barely adequate terms, what has been magnificently obvious for many years. His performances on stage and on the screen, which have ranged from farce to tragedy, from musical comedy to Shakespeare, easily qualify him as one of the giant figures of the American theater.

Winner of a Tony Award, an Academy Award, a New York Drama Critics Award, and honorary degrees from five universities; a child prodigy at the piano, a Princeton freshman at age sixteen, and a onetime budding architect—here is a man fulfilled, and fulfilling.

Born José Vincente Ferrer y Cintrón in Santurce, Puerto Rico, in 1912, young José was brought to live in the United States when he was six, where he attended public and private schools and showed such skill at music that it was felt he would someday be a concert pianist.

He matriculated at Princeton when he was fifteen but spent a year in a Swiss school when the university felt he was still a trifle too young to become an undergraduate.

When he finally did enter Princeton, James Stewart and Joshua Logan were among his fellow students. Ferrer amused himself by taking part in collegiate productions and by organizing a band, The Pied Pipers, that played for proms and other university functions.

Ferrer studied architecture at Princeton, and when he received his bachelor's degree in 1933, he went on to Columbia, fully intending to win his master's degree preparatory to a career of teaching.

But Columbia, as he would explain later, was too close to Broadway, and the stage beckoned. After a season in summer stock, he made his professional debut in the Broadway production of *A Slight Case of Murder*. He had one line.

But from the obscure beginning blossomed a career of unparalleled success. From small parts came bigger parts, from one-line roles came stardom in *Brother Rat* and *Charley's Aunt* and the brilliant somber part of Iago in *Othello*.

The role Ferrer is most associated with is that of Cyrano de Bergerac in Rostand's romantic classic, which he interpreted with sensitivity on Broadway in 1946 and on the screen in 1950. The former won him a Tony, the latter an Oscar.

By then he had already won an Academy nomination for his first movie role as the Dauphin in *Joan of Arc* and would be nominated again for his memorable portrait of the artist Toulouse Lautrec in *Moulin Rouge*.

Meanwhile, the restless genius established the New York Center Repertory Theatre, which presented everything from Chekhov to O'Neill, and branched out into directing and producing both plays and movies. Ferrer even wrote one or two as well.

Ferrer produced, directed, and starred in *The Shrike* on Broadway, which won him the best-acting award of the New York Drama Critics in 1952.

His list of credits is formidable both on the stage and in films, but Ferrer is no stranger either to concert performances. In 1964 he sang one aria by Marc Blitzstein at New York's Philharmonic Hall.

He has starred on Broadway in Noël Coward's musical *The Girl Who Came to Supper* and has toured the country in such musicals as *Little Me, Around the World in Eighty Days,* and *A Funny Thing Happened on the Way to the Forum.*

The range of Ferrer's talents, the wide variety of acting challenges he has accepted—from pratfall comedy to stark tragedy—has been the hallmark of his career, moving Nathaniel Benchley to write, "Just for fun I'd like to see José play *Little Women*. I'll bet he could do it."

As a more serious testimonial to Ferrer's genius, in 1967 the Pan American Union Secretariat General of the Organization of American States awarded the great actor a special bronze plaque in recognition of his rare contribution to the theatrical and motion-picture arts in the Americas.

Bishop Patrick Flores

Bishop Patrick Flores

When Patrick Fernández Flores announced to his local priests that he, too, wanted to enter the priesthood, they smiled. Here was a high-school dropout with, at best, a spotty education; here was a boy who worked as a farm laborer, who had spent seemingly as much time picking cotton as he had reading books. "They never encouraged me," he recalls now. "They kept putting me off." But he would show them the depth of his commitment in ways the clergymen could never imagine.

Patrick Flores not only became a priest, but, within fifteen years, at age forty, was auxiliary bishop of San Antonio, Texas—one of the youngest men ever named bishop, and the only Mexican-American among the church's 250 U.S. prelates.

It was a long step from farm hand to the Catholic clergy, but Bishop Flores would remark years later that the circumstances of his youth, including both the poverty and the hard work, only helped him become a better priest.

Patrick was one of nine children in the family. He was born in the Houston area, and as an infant migrated right along with his parents, brothers, and sisters to north Texas to pick cotton. He remembers times of racial slurs—when some restaurants wouldn't serve Mexican-Americans—and times when the family had to sleep in barns.

Bishop Flores' father was illiterate, and it seemed for a while that he might be too. Farm work filled his young life. From grades one through eight, he never had more than four or five months' schooling a year. When he began the tenth

grade, his father scraped together enough money to buy a
farm, and the boy dropped out of school to help.

For three years, as he worked to help make the farm pay,
Flores thought about entering the priesthood. When he talked
to the local priests and found no encouragement, he went to
a nun. She took him to the bishop in Galveston, who offered
not only encouragement but also money. The bishop would
pay Flores' way through high school.

It was a confirmation of his decision. Young Flores finished
high school at age twenty—at the top of the class—and then
entered a seminary to study for the priesthood. When he
finally began his work, he was only one of two Mexican-
Americans out of 220 priests in the Houston-Galveston dio-
cese.

Father Flores, troubled by that realization, began asking
questions. "For four-hundred years Mexicans have been
Catholics, but the church has had very few Mexican-American priests. Why?" It was answered only indirectly.

For meanwhile the chicano movement had taken hold in
the United States, and a combination of the movement,
Father Flores' provocative questions, and his own obvious
abilities as a priest assisted his rise to the position of auxiliary
bishop of San Antonio in 1970.

A popular priest who offered mariachi Masses (parishoners,
at first skeptical, soon overcrowded his church), Father Flores
was an equally popular bishop. The seven-thousand-capacity
convention center in San Antonio was used for his consecration ceremonies, and posters outside said "Viva Nuestro
Obispo Chicano!"

A mariachi band furnished the music here too, and guests
included labor leader César Chávez, activist José Ángel
Gutiérrez, and Bishop Sergio Méndez Arceo of Cuernavaca,
Mexico.

"The guest list alone," a newspaper columnist wrote,
"showed how involved Bishop Flores is in the problems of the
Mexican-American, the farm worker, and the young."

He added, "The consecration of Patricio Flores, a former
Texas migrant worker, as bishop of the Catholic Church,
indicates once more the church's growing sensitivity to the
chicano movement. It gave one hope that an ideal, like the
Catholic church, can still bring people together."

It presented too the determination and dedication of a
young man who, toiling under a hot Texas sun, decided he
had something more to offer society.

Antonio Frasconi

Antonio Frasconi

When Antonio Frasconi discovered at age twelve that he loved to draw, his mother admonished him for his "daring." Art, she had decided, was something far beyond their ken, an undertaking that was restricted to the level of the gods. For her son to aspire to this plateau, she believed, was somehow blasphemous, or at least terribly presumptuous. He felt otherwise.

Since then, the determined Frasconi—though in adolescence he was forced to practice his art as "something naughty, something hidden"—has become one of the world's most respected graphic artists and has been credited with the current revival of the woodcut in the United States.

He has translated the everyday subjects of the land into a style that combines representational portrayal with sophisticated vision: the color of the California wine country, the endless vegetable fields of the great Central Valley, the farms of Vermont, the shores of Long Island Sound, the markets of New York City.

Frasconi has become an artist of the people.

Born in 1919 in Buenos Aires, young Antonio's family moved to Montevideo early in his youth. It was here that he first began to draw, and, parental admonitions notwithstanding, he attended art school at night while working in his family's restaurant during the day. The school's main interest, he recalls, was copying plaster casts, and Antonio quickly lost his enthusiasm for the undertaking.

But then he remembers seeing his first Gauguin woodblocks at a loan exhibition from the Louvre, and something happened. "I was really shaking," he would say years later. This was *art*. This was his destiny.

Not that he turned immediately to that medium and to fame. For Frasconi there were long years of learning his craft, intermingled with jobs in the restaurant, with the government drawing graphs, and with a satirical newspaper drawing political cartoons. He even attended a school of architecture for a year.

Then at age twenty Frasconi had his first one-man show, an exhibition of drawings in Montevideo. A few years later, while apprenticed to a commercial printer, he began experimenting with the creative use of graphic media. This evolved into an exhibition of his woodcuts, and the artist Frasconi truly emerged into public view.

Since then, his name has become synonymous with the woodcut. He has had more than sixty one-man shows in the United States, Europe, and Latin America, and three major retrospective exhibitions at U.S. museums.

Additionally, Frasconi has designed and illustrated widely distributed, sometimes prize-winning books for both children and adults, magazine covers, Christmas cards, calendars, record-album covers, and book jackets.

In 1963 his design was chosen for a United States postage stamp that was reprinted 120 million times.

The tremendous amount of Frasconi's work is deliberate for personal as well as commercial reasons. He believes that the woodcut is "within the range of all people," and he has kept his prices low, often almost subsidizing collectors, in order to bring his art into as many homes as possible.

His work has won praise from many sources. A year after he came to New York in 1945, his first one-man show in the United States was acclaimed by *Print* magazine: "Certainly it is stimulating to find an artist who is capable of being of his time without being either insignificantly abstract or obviously representational."

Time called him "The U.S.'s foremost woodcut artist," and the curator of the New York Public Library wrote, "He hews into the wood like a sculptor into stone."

Frasconi has pursued social themes as well as themes depicting man at his work, and has illustrated the works of poets Walt Whitman and García Lorca. Critics have stood in awe of the new effects he has achieved in size, mood, and color.

The scope of his art continues to grow. And Antonio Frasconi continues to dare.

Dr. Antonio Gasset

Dr. Antonio Gasset

When it was announced in the fall of 1972 that Dr. Antonio Gasset, a Cuban refugee, had developed a technique to restore near-perfect vision to ten persons declared legally blind, no one was really surprised. It was the kind of achievement the medical world had come to expect from its genius ophthalmologist.

Antonio Gasset's career is filled with honors, and his discovery of a heat technique to treat a blinding corneal condition called keratoconus was simply an application of the expertise that has brought him recognition over the years since he fled Fidel Castro's Cuba.

Born in Havana in 1936, Dr. Gasset received his Bachelor of Science degree from the Colegio de Belén in 1954, then attended the University of Havana Medical School for the next six years. It was shortly thereafter that he left Cuba.

His first job in the United States was as a lab technician for the Retina Foundation in Boston. It was then that Dr. Gasset decided to specialize in ophthalmology. He worked as a research assistant and then was a corneal fellow of the foundation until 1967.

Gasset began taking graduate courses in ophthalmology at Harvard that same year, and then for the following three years specialized at the University of Florida, where he was a trainee in ophthalmology and, later, chief of the university's contact-lens clinic.

In 1971 Dr. Gasset took his first teaching job with the University of Florida's College of Medicine. He became an assistant professor of ophthalmology, a position he was holding when, at the age of thirty-six, he led a team of six to the discovery of a treatment for keratoconus.

Honors began piling up for Dr. Gasset just after he received his medical degree from Boston University in 1966. In successive years he won an award for the best research paper at Boston's St. Elizabeth's Hospital, the Hunter Romaine Award of the Association of Ophthalmologists, and the Physician's Recognition Award of the American Medical Association.

The same year that he began his teaching career, he was awarded the Rudolph Ellender Medical Foundation first annual honors for meritorious achievements and outstanding medical contributions.

The following year, 1972, he was twice honored—his second Physician's Recognition Award of the American Medical Association and the Premio Juan J. Ramos.

Since 1964 Dr. Gasset has authored or co-authored an incredible fifty-one articles on eye diseases and their treatment.

But his real accomplishment came with the breakthrough discovery that involved treating a diseased cornea with a pencil-slim probe.

Ten persons who had been declared legally blind, with vision of 20-200 or worse, volunteered for the new treatment. And in a paper presented before the American Academy of Ophthalmologists and Otolaryngologists in Dallas, Dr. Gasset revealed that all of the patients had recovered normal or near-normal sight.

The technique—its scientific name shortened to TKP—takes less than a minute, and is now being considered as a potential treatment for other eye problems.

Dr. Gasset, a man who turned the necessity to flee from his homeland Cuba into a study benefiting all mankind, is cautious. He says only that the process will take more study before its ultimate benefits are known.

Meanwhile, he is a fellow of the National Eye Institute and is already involved in new research for the benefit of all.

Congressman Henry B. González

Congressman Henry B. González

In 1957 the first Mexican-American to be seated in the Texas State Senate in 110 years stood. His name was Henry B. González, and he had risen to speak in opposition to ten "race bills" introduced before the legislature. The talk became a historic thirty-six-hour filibuster that helped defeat eight of the bills and projected the freshman state senator into the forefront of a growing fight for human rights.

It was not the first time that González had spoken out on behalf of racial and ethnic equality, and it would not be the last. But the occasion was notable for its daring and for the prophetic quality of his message long before the ghettos and the barrios would explode in flames. He told his fellow Texans, "It may be some can chloroform their consciences. But if we fear long enough, we hate; and if we hate long enough, we fight."

González would repeat that phrase many times in many ways during a long career of public service that eventually took him into the United States Congress, for he has been a man concerned not only with the need for social equality but also with the dangers implicit in *in*equality.

González was born in San Antonio, Texas, in 1916. His parents had fled from the Mexican revolution five years earlier. His father had been the mayor of a village in the state of Durango.

Young Henry was subjected early to the injustices he would later fight in the halls of legislature. He was barred from many places reserved "for whites only" and called "greaser" with impunity. "I spent two years in the first grade because I couldn't speak English," he remembers. "I was in the second grade before I realized I wasn't a Mexican. A teacher looked at my records and said, 'You're an American.' After that I wondered: What am I?"

An ambitious boy, Henry began working when he was only ten and became acutely aware of himself and the conditions around him. It was during those formative years that he told himself, "This is my land. I'm part of it. Why should I be an alien? I was born here."

Firm in that conviction and determined to someday instill it in others, González worked his way into the University of Texas but was forced to drop out when his jobs ended. Later he received his law degree at St. Mary's University School of Law.

Instead of practicing law, however, González quickly revealed his concern for society's outcasts by becoming a juvenile probation officer. He returned to the work as chief probation officer after the Second World War (where he served as a civilian with both Army and Navy intelligence), but quit when a county judge refused to let him hire a black to serve on an equal basis with the rest of the staff.

In 1950 González was elected to the San Antonio City Council, where he sponsored an ordinance that ended segregation in the city's recreational facilities, and six years later he was elected to the state Senate, achieving prominence with his filibustering fight against the ten race bills.

González was reelected to the Senate in 1960, but the following year won a special election for a vacant seat in the U.S. House of Representatives, where he has served ever since.

Always a fighter against segregation and exploitation of the poor, he expanded that fight as a congressman into new areas of concern—adult basic education, civil-service salary increases, benefits for farm workers, income-tax-exemption increases.

At the same time, González became active on behalf of the Peace Corps and conservation, and began speaking out for the need in this country for "freedom from the compulsion to conform."

He warned against war profiteering, opposed the bracero program of farm labor importation from Mexico, and urged statehood for the District of Columbia.

But despite all of his other legislative activities, González remains in the forefront of the fight for social equality, noting with irony that, where once he was attacked by right-wing extremists for doing too much, he is now often attacked by left-wing extremists for not doing enough.

"What saddens me most of all," he says, "is not that I am personally an issue; it is that the issue, the real issue, is not being addressed at all: How do we defeat poverty and hopelessness and despair?"

Horacio Gutiérrez

Horacio Gutiérrez

They said it in Los Angeles, they said it in New York, they said it in Amsterdam, and they said it in Moscow. "Horacio Gutiérrez," wrote the critics, "is a name to remember." The words were almost identical, though the writers were separated by continents and oceans—for here was a young concert pianist with special gifts, and their unanimous acclaim for his awesome talent is understandable.

In the Netherlands they call Gutiérrez "the Piano Lion," in Montreal "the Wizard of the Keyboard," in Santa Monica "*the* pianist of our time."

Wrote a Miami columnist with almost breathless incredulity, "In technique, dynamics, characterization, and comprehensive style, his is a huge performance that would reduce a lesser piano to rubble."

And Horacio Gutiérrez is but twenty-five years old.

Born in Havana, Cuba, in 1958, young Horacio's mother was a music teacher and his father a music lover, but neither pushed their son to the piano. He was, without persuasion, tapping out melodies on a keyboard when he was two. By the time he was three he was taking piano lessons because he wanted to; a year later he was performing in recitals; and at age eleven he appeared as a soloist with the Havana Symphony Orchestra.

There was no need to persuade. Genius seeks its own level.

Political turmoil in Cuba disrupted the family's life when the forces of Fidel Castro overthrew the Batista government. At first, Horacio remembers, his father was ecstatic, but eventually saw Castro's turn to Communism as a betrayal of the revolution. They fled to the United States in 1961.

"It made me want to be very nonpolitical," the astute young artist says today. "You can do that in music because music is always the same, always beautiful. Governments change, but music remains as it was written."

The family reached Miami almost penniless, and there was no piano for Gutiérrez to play. But when his genius was revealed, a Baptist church offered the use of their instrument, and lessons were given free of charge. Later, when the Gutiérrezes moved to Los Angeles, pianos were lent willingly to the musical prodigy.

Fame came fast thereafter. Just five years after his family left Cuba, Horacio was chosen by Leonard Bernstein as soloist for the New York Philharmonic's Young People's Concerts. A year later he won first prize in the San Francisco Symphony auditions, and the famed Juilliard School offered him a scholarship.

Other honors followed, but the star of Gutiérrez's greatness shone brightest in the summer of 1970. He finished second in the piano division of the prestigious IV International Tchaikovsky Competition in Moscow in a grueling twenty-two-day contest with two hundred other entrants from thirty-five nations.

He was only twenty-one at the time.

Since then, Horacio Gutiérrez—the name to remember—has played across the United States and around the world to standing ovations and awestricken critics.

Once, playing with a severely cut finger, he was praised by the Houston *Post* as "clearly much more than a mere keyboard virtuoso; he is a great musician." Even the sedate *New York Times,* noting Gutiérrez's Manhattan debut, was astonished by his "breadth, continuity, and communication of personal involvement—a combination that comes only to a full-fledged artist. He is obviously headed for a major career."

Booked years in advance, Gutiérrez is *already* involved in a major career—one that may prove him the most accomplished concert pianist of the age, with a repertoire ranging from Haydn to Prokofiev. And this is only the beginning. Most critics agree that his best years lie ahead.

But the superlatives showered over him have not trapped the Cuban-American artist (he became a naturalized U.S. citizen in 1967) in the isolation of arrogance that imprisons so many who achieve success. His co-artists acclaim his amiability as enthusiastically as they acclaim his style.

Gutiérrez himself speaks of his adopted country as "still the golden land of opportunity" and his audiences as the ultimate judges of his music.

"I demand a great deal of myself, and I don't blame poor performances on anyone else. You can win ten competitions, and it still just means you were the best one there. It doesn't mean you're a great artist. The only thing that matters is you and the audience. I play for them."

José Ángel Gutiérrez

José Ángel Gutiérrez

The dream of José Ángel Gutiérrez, a young Mexican-American social activist and educator, is to see the emergence of a national Raza Unida, a united people's party, as a major political force in the United States. And if the dream seems far-fetched, consider the case of Crystal City.

A town of ten thousand in south Texas, Crystal City—with its own hostilities and its own apathies—was undistinguished in the arena of ethnic politics until the spring of 1970. It was then that a group of chicanos led by Gutiérrez founded La Raza Unida.

Through it, they won control of the government and the school board in Crystal City, as well as political offices in two other nearby towns, and the party was beginning to flex its muscle throughout the entire Southwest.

Gutiérrez was born in Crystal City in 1944 and received political-science degrees from Texas A&I and a master's in political science from St. Mary's College in San Antonio. At the present time he is in the process of obtaining his Ph.D. in government at the University of Texas in Austin.

In the late 1960's he became first president of the new Mexican-American Youth Organization (MAYO) and developed a militancy that often unnerved his more moderate contemporaries.

A scholarly-appearing man, Gutiérrez has often surprised those around him by vowing, perhaps in media-oriented rhetoric, that "We will eliminate the gringo"—causing at least one prominent Mexican-American congressman to shudder at what he considered the young militant's "reverse racism."

Gutiérrez's success, and the success of La Raza Unida in Crystal City, rests partially at least on a MAYO conference held the year preceding the 1970 Crystal City election.

It was there that the Plan de Aztlán was adopted, referring to the legendary homeland of the Aztec Indians in far-northern Mexico, in what is now the southwestern United States.

The young delegates at the MAYO conference chose the name Aztlán for what they consider a separate chicano nation existing in the Southwest. But in spirit it sparked a political fire that blazed first in Crystal City.

Gutiérrez went on to help organize the town's La Raza Unida, and was himself elected to the school board, eventually becoming board president, in the chicanos' political landslide.

The party worked not only for votes in Crystal City but for converts. Its members helped Spanish-speaking persons through the state's complex voter regulations, organized community classes for the predominant Mexican population, and created a kind of chicano Chamber of Commerce to work with the local businessmen.

The purpose of organizing La Raza Unida, Gutiérrez would explain time and again, was to break a "cycle of chicano depression" in south Texas. "The keys to breaking this cycle are to be found not only in political and educational reforms, but in economic and ethnic identity."

Crystal City's schools were almost totally overhauled under the new regime. The teaching staff in a two-year period went from sixty-five-percent Anglo to seventy-percent chicano. Mexican-Americans control *every* department in the town, from the police force to the housing authority.

And since that 1970 election, which saw fifteen members of Raza Unida elected, the party now has thirty officeholders scattered throughout parts of Texas.

At its first national convention in El Paso, the party spearheaded by Gutiérrez drew a stunning 2,500 delegates from eighteen states. Gutiérrez himself expressed amazement. "Now chicanos all over Texas want to pull a Crystal City of their own," he told the press, referring to an earlier statement: "Aztlán had to start somewhere. Why not Crystal City?"

Now Gutiérrez dreams the dream of a nationally influential Raza Unida, and no one is laughing at the husky, bespectacled activist. Noted one supporter with admiration, "José has learned the Anglos' game of politics. And he's beating the hell out of them at it."

José Limón

José Limón

The great dancer-choreographer José Limón once said of his work, "I want to dig beneath empty formalisms, displays of technical virtuosity, and the slick surface to probe the human entity for the powerful, often crude, beauty of the gesture that speaks of man's humanity." Few artists ever achieve what they set out to do, but in a display of grace that dazzled the world, José Limón did.

He was, by one measure, the male dancer of our age, and by another the leading spiritual force in modern dance in the United States. Both as a performer and a choreographer, Limón grappled with the great issues of the world, interpreting with genius and sensitivity the endless struggle between good and evil that has characterized mankind's existence on Earth.

One of his themes dealt with the torment of treachery—the execution for treason of Ethel and Julius Rosenberg—and another with the horror of the Second World War that drove families from their homes in flaming Europe.

José Arcadio Limón was born in 1908 in Sinaloa, Mexico. The family moved to Arizona when he was seven, and later to Los Angeles, where he grew up. From his father, a musician, the boy inherited a deep love for music, and from his devout mother he gained a regard for the beauty of church ritual. Both were to affect him.

Limón started out to be a painter, an art he pursued both at UCLA and at the New York School of Design. But painting, he found, was not for him, and he drifted for a while without purpose.

Then, in the late 1920's, he saw a performance by the modern dancer Harald Kreutzberg. In Limón's words, "What I saw simply and irrevocably changed my life. I saw the dance as a vision of ineffable power."

He enrolled for classes at the Doris Humphrey–Charles Weidman Studio. By 1930 he was dancing in a chorus on Broadway, and by 1931 he was choreographing his own compositions.

Limón choreographed and danced in many Broadway shows at first, then concluded that "the commercial form and the serious form of dance were incompatible" and devoted himself thereafter to concert dance. His first recognition as a choreographer of special promise came in 1937, when he was awarded a fellowship at the Bennington School of Dance.

In the years that followed, his fame grew as his talent blossomed, and a little more than a decade after he began dancing, a critic was writing that Limón had taken his place "unquestionably as one of the important artists in the contemporary dance."

After two years in the Army, Limón formed a trio and placed it under the artistic direction of the great Doris Humphrey, his mentor and adviser. The group produced Limón's and Miss Humphrey's works for the next thirteen years. One of her compositions, *Lament for Ignacio Sánchez Mejías,* based on a Garcia Lorca poem, became one of Limón's most celebrated dance roles.

There were others of equal magnificence: *The Story of Mankind,* a satiric creation that traced the evolution of man from cave to penthouse and back to cave; *Day on Earth,* a dance of family love; *The Traitor,* an allegory that touched on the tragedy of the Rosenbergs; and *The Exiles,* about those driven from their homes by war.

The José Limón Company traveled the world under an international cultural exchange program: to Latin America, Europe, the Near and Far East. He lunched with President John Kennedy and danced for President Lyndon Johnson.

Once he was offered directorship of the National Academy of Dance in Mexico, but declined, preferring the independent life of an unsubsidized dancer in the United States; though he did join the faculty of the great Juilliard School. In 1960 Limón received an honorary Doctor of Fine Arts degree from Wesleyan University, and in 1964 he was chosen artistic director of the American Dance Theatre.

In the closing days of his life, José Limón asked, "What are we here on Earth for if not to illuminate our experiences for ourselves and for others?" That he did so magnificently is legend.

Mr. Limón died of natural causes in December, 1972.

Trini López

Trini López

When Trini López sang "If I Had a Hammer," the audiences in the nightclubs where he performed invariably turned on. The power of style and rhythm bound them into a single enthusiastic, hand-clapping unit, but there was something more too, and it was in the lyrics: "I would hammer out love between my brothers and my sisters, all over this land."

Brotherhood was a compelling theme in that difficult year of 1963, and Trini made its message ring across America. This rising star, a young Mexican-American in an Anglo society, epitomized what the lyricist was trying to say, and the impact was not lost on those who listened.

Trini's recording of the song eventually sold four and a half million copies. The poor boy from a Texas barrio had come a long way.

Trinidad López III was born in Dallas on May 15, 1937, one of six children who, with the parents, occupied a one-room house in the city's Mexican section.

He remembers barely enough food for the family, the amount always determined by his parents' ability to get whatever work they could. "They worked and struggled together just to survive," he recalls. "They plowed fields together. My mother washed clothes in the neighborhood. You can't imagine how hard it was."

Trini was only eleven when, with his father's encouragement, he decided on a career in music. The elder López, who had loved the guitar from his own childhood, saved twelve dollars and bought one now for his eldest son. It was all Trini needed.

He taught himself to play and sing, and eventually formed

his own group. At first, they worked for almost nothing in the
restaurants of the barrio, but Trini's quality would not be
denied. He went on to El Pango Club in Dallas and to other
big clubs throughout the Southwest.

By 1960, when he was twenty-three, Trini felt that he was
ready for the big time, for the entertainment capital of the
world—Hollywood.

The group's reputation in the Southwest was big, their con-
fidence high. They went to California filled with optimism.

It didn't work out as they had expected. Only Trini was
able to find a job; there was nothing available for them as a
group. Out of desperation, he took it. Trini López, the soloist,
was born.

The engagement at Ye Little Club was to have lasted two
weeks. It lasted a year. From there, it was on to the celebrated
P.J.'s and other nightclubs in the Los Angeles area.

Don Costa, the musical director of Reprise Records, heard
him at P.J.'s, taped his act, and played it for the princi
owner of the company, Frank Sinatra. The great singer re
ognized a fellow stylist and signed López to an exclusi
contract.

That was in 1963. Things had been happening fast for Trini,
but now they were happening even faster.

Reprise released his first album, *Trini Lopez at P.J.'s,*
and it sold a million copies. One of the tunes in it was "If I
Had a Hammer," which as a single became an international
hit.

From there, it was on to standing-room-only audiences for
Trini across the face of Europe. He had earned about half a
million dollars by then, and his weekly salary was five thousand dollars.

In mid-June he made his New York debut with his own
eleven-man orchestra that included his brother Jesse, and the
tough Manhattan critics were unanimous in their praise of the
young man from the Texas barrio.

Trini López had become a superstar in every sense of the
word. He was doing what the lyrics of his first big hit promised
that someday he would do. By deed and example, by talent
and verve, he was ringing out love between his brothers and
his sisters, all over this land.

Judge Harold R. Medina

Judge Harold R. Medina

In a legal career that has spanned sixty-one years, Federal Judge Harold R. Medina has often been called upon to illustrate the most noble elements of American jurisprudence: by defending a man accused of treason in the Second World War; by presiding over the historic and chaotic trial of eleven Communists charged with conspiring to advocate violent overthrow of the United States government; and by championing the cause of a free press at a time of adversity.

They have not been easy times for the distinguished jurist. During the 1942 treason trial, which he took without charge to prove that justice was real, he was spat upon as pro-Nazi. Presiding over the Cold War conspiracy trial of those eleven Communists—called one of the greatest court cases in American history—he had to bear abuse as few judges have.

And now, at a day when the integrity of the First Amendment is under attack by efforts to muzzle the press, he is in the forefront of a movement to preserve that freedom at all costs.

Harold R. Medina was born in Brooklyn in 1888 of Mexican and Dutch ancestry. He attended public school, a military academy, and then was graduated with highest honors in French from Princeton University. Thereafter he was graduated from Columbia University Law School, where he had earned straight A's with one ironic exception: a B in trial evidence, an area in which he would someday excel. He was accepted to the New York bar in 1912.

Attorney Medina's career began with an eight-dollar-a-week job with a law firm, expanded to include tutoring of as many as sixteen hundred law students at a time in rented halls that were filled to overflowing, and then added a teaching job at Columbia. Later he gave up teaching for private practice, commanding fees as high as fifty-thousand dollars.

It was during this period of his growing reputation that he defended a man charged with treason, a case he won on appeal. "I took the case without fee to prove that equal justice for all is a real and not a phony principle of American law," he said later. "My friends wouldn't talk to me. I was spit on in court."

In 1947 President Truman appointed Medina to the U.S. District Court in New York, and eighteen months later he was presiding over what became one of the longest and most important trials in the history of the United States.

Eleven top Communists were eventually convicted of conspiring to overthrow the government, and their attorneys were cited for contempt in what had become a bitter test of Judge Medina's forbearance and justice's imperviousness to abuse.

It was a trying time. Medina suffered insults both in and out of the courtroom, pickets hooted their opposition out front, and guards stayed with him during the entire nine months of the ordeal.

There were days, the judge recalls, when he felt he could take no more. Once, especially, "I was pretty close to gone, and I had to lie down. Whether I'd ever get back into that courtroom, I didn't know. I did the most sincere and most fervent praying that I had ever done in my life."

But return to the courtroom he did, and when it was all over, Medina was able to smile and say, "Strange as it may seem, I'm still glad that I'm a judge."

Later the *Los Angeles Times* observed, "In a sense, the Communists tried to put our judicial system on trial. Judge Medina became the symbol of that system, and he acquitted himself with dignity, patience, courage, and a profound sense of justice."

In 1951 he was promoted to the U.S. Circuit Court and retired in 1958. But he has continued working without interruption with the special designation of senior judge.

More recently Judge Medina has involved himself in the growing effort to curb press coverage of court trials. He has called it a violation of constitutional freedom and has urged the news media to "fight like tigers" and "not give an inch" where the First Amendment is at stake.

In an aside that might include reference to his own brilliant career, the judge added, "I know we'll get cussed out for it. The minute you do anthing worth doing, you get cussed out."

Lieutenant Governor Roberto Mondragón

Carlos Montoya

Carlos Montoya

Carlos Montoya was born with music in his heart. He absorbed the melodies of his land the way most children pick up language, and refined it into an art form that "liberated" the flamenco guitar and made him one of the foremost musicians in the world. When Carlos Montoya plays, there is magic in the air.

He was born in Madrid to a family of full-blooded Spanish gypsies; his mother was an amateur guitarist who began teaching Carlos how to make music when he was still an infant. His father died when he was two.

It became apparent early in his childhood that there was little he had to be taught, for music seemed a part of his whole being, even though he could not, and still cannot, read it. By the time he was fourteen he was skilled enough to accompany singers and dancers in the cafés of Spain.

Montoya's devotion to music was a consuming devotion, and whatever else he did in life, music remained his prime concern. Ordinary work would, by necessity, occupy his days, but the guitar held his every second of attention thereafter.

Even during three years in the Spanish Army, serving tough duty in uneasy Morocco, Carlos played the guitar whenever he could, to whoever would listen, and often when no one would listen. Night after steamy night he would fill the encampment with the sound of music.

After his discharge, Montoya returned to the cafés of Madrid, but not for long. The famous Antonia Merce, "La Argentina," heard him play and asked him to tour with her group. He traveled with them throughout Europe for three years, then joined with the dancer Vicente Escudero for a short while, and finally toured with the troupe of La Teresina through the United States and the Far East.

His fame was growing. He was offered teaching jobs and money. Films were made of his playing, as though visual study of his movements would capture the awesome magnitude of his talent.

Montoya was touring in the United States when the Second World War broke out. He stayed, married Sallie MacLean, an American citizen, and then himself acquired citizenship. The night that he did, he played for President Truman.

Shortly after the war's end, the great guitarist took an important step. It was time, he decided, to determine if the function of the flamenco guitar was only to accompany a singer or dancer, or whether it might stand on its own.

To test his contention that it could stand alone, Montoya, at age forty-three, set out to give solo concerts.

At first he was lucky to attract an audience of two hundred. They were accustomed to singers and dancers with their flamenco guitar. They could not understand yet how much musical power there existed in one man with one instrument.

But Carlos Montoya's was a compelling gift, and soon the style and the strength of his music began once more to attract attention.

A reviewer for the *New York Times* suggested that Montoya's guitar created "such picturesque noises as tambourines, the stamping of heels in a dance, the clatter of castanets, snapping fingers, and even the snare drums of a military band."

He was duplicating on a single guitar the effects usually produced by an entire flamenco troupe.

Carlos Montoya's reputation was by now beyond the critics, even those who urged a softer style, asking, "Surely Spanish gypsies are not *always* on the front burner?"

His music, he insists, is from the heart, and cannot be compromised. "It is very deep music, very fundamental. It is not intellectual. It is what we feel. It is not folklore, because it cannot be played by all the people, but only by a small number. You can put some of it on paper, but that is all. Some of it vanishes when you do."

In 1966 Montoya and a collaborator composed history's first flamenco suite for a full orchestra, and it was performed by the St. Louis Symphony Orchestra. He looks back upon it as a high point in his long and brilliant career.

Senator Joseph Montoya

Senator Joseph Montoya

The boy wonder of New Mexico politics began his career at age twenty-one with a deep commitment to human rights and consumer protection. Thirty-seven years later, now one of the most important members of the United States Senate, Joseph Montoya has not lost what may have seemed to some the idealism of youth. Elevation of the human condition is still his main concern.

The only Mexican-American member of the legislative upper house, Senator Montoya has sponsored specific bills and has campaigned generally on behalf of consumerism, involving both foods and hazardous toys and fabrics. He has also been crucially concerned with environmental quality and has worked hard on behalf of the United States's twelve million Spanish-speaking citizens.

A native of Sandoval County, New Mexico, young Joseph attended grade school in Bernalillo, New Mexico, and then Regis College in Denver. At Georgetown University, Montoya received his Doctor of Jurisprudence degree and became interested in politics.

Armed with his law degree, Montoya ran for and was elected to the New Mexico House of Representatives. At twenty-one, he was the youngest person in the history of the state ever to win the office. Reelected two years later, he became Democratic majority leader of the House.

Montoya served twelve years in the House and state Senate, and eight years as lieutenant governor of the state. In 1957 he was elected to the first of four successive terms in the U.S. House of Representatives.

In 1964 Montoya was elected to the United States Senate. He was reelected in 1970.

A member of several important committees—including Appropriations and Public Works—Senator Montoya has been a firm believer in the idea of self-help and has encouraged deprived youngsters to educate themselves and has also promoted cooperative education, by which employers help pay for their workers' schooling.

Senator Montoya has been especially active in upgrading the nation's Spanish-speaking people. He is committed personally and politically to enhancing the pluralistic cultural, lingual, and ethnic heritage of the Southwest, as well as in other parts of the nation.

Additionally, he has urged a single standard of justice, law enforcement, job opportunities, promotion, and hiring by the Federal civil service, and has attacked the pockets of discrimination still existing against Hispanos in the United States.

Senator Montoya has authored the Bilingual Education Act, a bill establishing the historic Cabinet Committee on Opportunities for Spanish-Speaking Americans, and legislation establishing the National Hispanic Heritage Week.

Internationally, the only Spanish-speaking member of the U.S. Senate has represented the United States at a number of inter-American conferences at the request of the President.

He has been a delegate to several annual Mexico–United States Interparliamentary Conferences and has played a significant role in advancing and strengthening relations between the two nations.

Senator Montoya was an ardent foe of the Vietnam war and advocated a swift phaseout of the American military commitment in Southeast Asia.

A believer in national security, he has nevertheless advocated less attention to war and more to those problems that burden all peoples of the United States.

Rita Moreno

Rita Moreno

Tiny Rita Moreno, weary of the mentality that endlessly type-cast her as "the Latin spitfire with flaring nostrils," left Hollywood in 1962 with an Oscar and a deep frustration. She would eventually lose the latter in a series of movies and stage performances that brought her success as an actress without the flaring nostrils. Rita Moreno, she set out to prove, could overcome a stereotype. *She could act.*

Not that there had ever been any question of her basic theatrical talent. She was born Rosa Dolores Alverio in Humacao, Puerto Rico; her parents brought her to New York when she was five, and by the time she was six she was taking dancing lessons. By the time she was seven, she was on stage.

That performance, as a Spanish dancer in a Greenwich Village nightclub, was the beginning of a career that has brought distinction to the pretty and multitalented Rita. Four years after her debut she turned professional with a five-dollar imitation of movie star Carmen Miranda at a New York bar mitzvah. Four years after that she won the bit part of a dancer in the play *Skydrift,* which lasted one week on Broadway.

There were endless hours of dancing lessons intermixed with jobs dubbing voices in films for export to Spanish-speaking countries, and even dramatic roles on radio shows. At night she worked in clubs.

The exhausting schedule began to pay off in 1949. She was offered her first movie role in a film about reform schools called *So Young, So Bad.* The following year she was signed for a part in her second stage play, *Signore Chicago.*

The play was a failure, but Rita's part in it was a success.

Louis B. Mayer saw her and offered her a contract with MGM. She was on her way to Hollywood.

There were many movies after that, from *Singin' in the Rain* to *The King and I,* but the film that won her the Oscar was *West Side Story.* She was named best supporting actress in 1962 for her portrayal of Anita.

"I stayed in Hollywood for another year after that," she said later. "But they offered me more Latin spitfire roles, which was mostly what I'd had before, The roles had nothing to do with real Latin women."

Frustrated, she fled the movie capital to prove elsewhere there was more in the talent of Rita Moreno than a "fiery half-breed" or a "Mexican hot tamale"—billings she had come to despise.

In London she was featured in Hal Prince's stage production of *She Loves Me.* In Chicago she was Serafina in *The Rose Tattoo,* a part that won her the Joseph Jefferson Award as the best actress in the city for that year. In New York she was a Jewish girl in *The Sign in Sidney Brustein's Window,* Sister Sharon in *Gantry,* and a suburban housewife in *Last of the Red Hot Lovers.*

There were movies, too: *Night of the Following Day* made in France with Marlon Brando, and finally the brilliant *Popi* with Alan Arkin that established her without doubt as a fine actress. She came back to Hollywood seven years after she left to do *Marlowe* with James Garner, but declined to stay.

Happily married, Rita Moreno continues to work in the field she loves, including television. She gives time to her own interests by appearing in the educational TV series *The Electric Company* and by belonging to the board of directors of Third World Cinema, a company interested in creating opportunities in the film industry for minority groups.

There have been other plays and other movies for the actress who abandoned temporary success to prove a point. She is disappointed that commercial television has not offered greater opportunities for Hispano-Americans, other than roles "for a quote-unquote villain with gold teeth." But, she adds, "I'll go on whistling 'America' and see if anything happens."

Armando Muñiz

Armando Muñíz

The message from Armando Muñíz—a North American welterweight boxing champion, a serious student of education, and an articulate spokesman for his people—is as compelling as it is uncomplicated: "Look at me."

He says it as often as he can to anyone who will listen, in classrooms and on the streets, to adoring fans and wary chicano militants. "Look at me," says Muñíz. "Anybody can get an education and make himself a better man. Everybody has problems. You can't quit. Just keep swing̣ing."

Armando Muñíz is a winner in a very real sense, as an amateur and then a professional boxer, and as a promising young schoolteacher. But the price of winning is hard work, and he makes that an important element of his message and his life.

When he was studying for his teaching credential and boxing at the same time, the deceptively gentle, soft-spoken Mando's day began at five in the morning and included two hours of road work before a full load of classes. Late in the afternoon there was a two-hour workout in the gym, and then often an exhibition fight after that. He wasn't usually home until after seven in the evening.

Later, as the North American welterweight boxing champion, it took a sixty-day suspension by the California Athletic Commission to get Muñíz to rest. He was suspended not for any infraction of the rules, but because he was boxing too often. "It is what you must do," he says with an easy smile, "to win."

Armando Muñíz was born in Chihuahua, Mexico, in 1947.

but his parents settled in southern California when he was still an infant. He attended high school in Los Angeles, went on to junior college, and then won a wrestling scholarship to UCLA.

Two years in the Army interrupted his education but paid off in his sports career. Muñíz became a champion boxer, winning All-Army and All-Service honors and emerging as the victor in forty-two out of forty-five matches, including some over Russia's best boxers in Moscow.

He toured the world as a blue-ribbon amateur champion and was the most popular member of the United States boxing team in the Mexico City Olympic Games, where he got as far as the quarterfinals. His total amateur record was an incredible seventy-two wins, five losses, and one tie.

Back in civilian life, the energetic Armando won his bachelor's degree in Spanish at California State College, Los Angeles, then immediately began work toward a master's degree and a secondary teaching credential. He had meanwhile married and was the father of two.

And, as if college and family-raising weren't enough, he turned professional boxer.

Muñíz says that he considers boxing a means to an end, not an end in itself. He has, in that sense, fought his way through school, supported a growing family, and even purchased a home for his parents. "It's a way of achieving something I dreamed of as a kid."

And he is willing to share his dreams even now with youngsters in the East Los Angeles barrio, telling them that if he could do it, they can do it. Chicano militants occasionally criticize his unwillingness to raise a fist in anger outside the ring.

"I tell them [the militants] what I really believe". Muñíz says, "that what I do as an individual reflects everyone else in my community. I know there are injustices and inequities. But how are you going to be against racism if you stay on a nationalistic track?"

The busy young boxer-student breaks training and sneaks out on his studies often enough to speak to service clubs also, because, as he says, "There are so many things to do. I want to do what I can to make it better for my people . . . better for everybody."

During one of his talks to some young people in an elementary school composed primarily of Mexican-American students. Muñíz tried to summarize his attitude and spark their hope: "In order to win, you must work. You must set goals. Complete this goal and go on to the one after that, and then the one after that." He might have added again: *"Look at me."*

Dr. Julián Nava

Dr. Julián Nava

When Julián Nava was in high school, his counselors advised him to be an automobile mechanic. It was a "realistic" assessment of a young Mexican-American's career opportunities in an Anglo society before the era of ethnic consciousness. But it was not a perceptive evaluation of the ultimate Julián Nava.

For a while, however, he accepted the notion that automotive mechanics might constitute his future. No one advised him to enter college. "I had always thought," he remembers, "that Anglos were smarter than Mexicans. Everybody knew that. And minority members learn it sooner than anybody else."

The immediate consideration of more education became a moot point with the Second World War. Nava went into the Navy during his last year of high school, and in basic training emerged as more an individual than a member of an oppressed minority.

"In boot camp it suddenly hit me that there were millions of people in this country who didn't give a damn *what* I was. For the first time I was just Julián."

The discovery was a turning point in his life, and Nava forever abandoned any thought of an automotive career. After the Navy he went on to win his Ph.D. at Harvard, assumed a professorship in history at southern California's San Fernando Valley State College, and won a place on the Los Angeles Board of Education by unseating a two-term incumbent.

Dr. Nava was born in the Boyle Heights area of East Los Angeles in 1927. His parents had fled to Texas to escape the revolution raging in Mexico, and then moved to California.

The young Julián spent hours in his father's barber shop (where the elder Nava also fashioned stringed musical instruments) to watch a fine artisan at work on the instruments and on hand-carved chess sets.

It became a kind of social center where the men gathered to talk politics. Nava believes today that the combination of politics and artisan excellence helped shape his attitudes in the arena of public conduct.

His career in high school was unspectacular. It wasn't until his discharge from the Navy as "just Julián" that the real Nava began to emerge.

He was elected student-body president at East Los Angeles Junior College, where he was an A student; won a scholarship to Pomona College, where he earned his B.A. degree; and then was awarded grants to Harvard, where he received both his M.A. and Ph.D.

In 1967, backed by a steering committee from every ethnic, religious, and geographic plateau of the sprawling metropolis, Dr. Nava won an unprecedented victory as a member of the Los Angeles Board of Education.

It was the first time in this century that a Mexican-American had campaigned for public office throughout the entire city and had won. His victory was an impressive fifty-three percent.

In 1971 (during which time he was serving as president of the school board) Dr. Nava ran for a second four-year term. And even though there were six candidates running against him, he took fifty-one percent of the vote in the *primary* election, thereby avoiding the necessity of a runoff later.

The victories were sweet for Julián Nava, because it took more than the vote of the minorities to put him in office. It took a concentration of support from even the staunchly conservative sections of the big city.

"It proves," he says, "that a Mexican-American can win office and become involved in civic life. A whole new social context exists in Los Angeles. New residents have swamped old prejudices. Being Mexican-American is now either a neutral or positive factor."

Dr. Nava, meanwhile, has set about building bridges of understanding between men, as angered by Mexican chauvinism as he is by Anglo chauvinism. Since his tenure in public office, the bridge has been crossed by many.

Frank Negrón

Frank Negrón

Frank Negrón is a man for all minorities. As director of New York City University's vast Affirmative Action Program, he is, by assignment and inclination, responsible for providing equal employment not only for Puerto Ricans, but also for women and for blacks and other minority groups in the system's twenty-unit complex. It is a job of no small undertaking, but Frank Negrón is no small man.

Born in the big city in 1928, Negrón received both his bachelor and master's degrees from NYU, and followed that up by attending New York Law School.

But even during his college years, he worked in the Puerto Rico Migration Division's community organization section in New York, helping to assimilate his recently arrived fellow Puerto Ricans into their new environment—guiding, consulting, and offering direct aid when necessary.

Simultaneously, he was lecturing *other* ethnic groups on the historical, cultural, and economic background of Puerto Rico, to better strengthen the bonds of understanding among all men.

Dropping out of law school, Negrón continued to fulfill what already seemed his destiny: helping. He joined the New York City Youth Board and for a year worked with potential young delinquents in the Bronx—with the always-dangerous street gangs—to reshape their attitudes and redirect their anti-social values into channels of personal worth and community development.

From there, still in his early thirties and already being recognized for his expertise in social programming, Negrón went on to the directorship of the Chelsea Neighborhood Conservation and Rehabilitation Project of the Hudson Guild.

He trained and supervised social-work students, college undergraduates, Peace Corps and VISTA workers, and directly coordinated the relocation of families living in overcrowded conditions, counseling them on their rights and obligations in their communities.

A few years later, Negrón took another giant step, this time as executive director of ASPIRA of America, the only professional Puerto Rican nonprofit education agency in the country. He quickly established city, state, and federal contacts and busied himself in the full-time job of telling the Puerto Rican story "stateside."

Negrón's movement into public service was inevitable, and in 1967 he was appointed deputy commissioner in the mayor's Office of Education Affairs in New York, the highest-ranking Puerto Rican educational official in the city.

Two years later, now committed to education, he became assistant director of the Center for Urban Education, the nation's largest educational laboratory experimenting in the development and implementation of community educational programs. Among Negrón's responsibilities was the coordination of activities in school districts with predominantly black and Puerto Rican children.

In 1971 Frank Negrón moved into his present position as director of the City University's Affirmative Action Program, seeking out equal employment opportunities for all minorities in both academic and nonacademic sections of the widespread university.

The program reaches even into campus construction projects, encouraging the recruitment and training of minority workers and developing programs to assure greater participation in university building plans by minority contractors and subcontractors.

To list Negrón's other achievements in the field of social betterment would fill another chapter. He co-founded the first bilingual program at City University, created the first leadership development program of the Puerto Rican Parents Foundation and the Puerto Rican Forum, and coordinated the first national hearings on equal educational opportunities for Puerto Ricans before a U.S. Senate committee.

In 1972 Negrón received the American Heritage Award

by the JFK Library for Minorities in recognition of his tireless effort in helping create new frontiers of understanding among all men.

Judge Philip Newman

Judge Philip Newman

Los Angeles Municipal Court Judge Philip Newman is proof of his own contention that a man can make it if he wants to. In fact, he insists, the struggle to mold shadows of ambition into substantive form—to make the dream come true—can temper and toughen the dream-seeker and make him someday better able to assist in a larger effort to help others.

Not that Newman, the only Mexican-born judge in the United States, rose to high position alone. A natural ambition to succeed was fired by the example of his remarkable father, who, one shattered life behind him, began a new career in a new land at middle age and set an example that his son would not soon forget.

Philip Newman, one of eight children, was born in Mexico City in 1916. His father was a German-born American citizen, his mother Mexican. They fled the political turmoil of Mexico in the late 1920's, leaving all but their barest possessions behind, and arrived in southern California without enough money to pay a month's rent.

The four young Newman sons went to work immediately to help support the family, almost taking over a Los Angeles intersection. Two of the boys, including Philip, sold newspapers on two of the corners, and the other brothers worked in service stations at the other two corners.

Their father, Bruno, had also taken a daytime job, but he had other plans as well. A successful mining engineer and political activist in Mexico, he was not content to settle permanently for menial employment in California. For six years he studied law at night, and in 1933—at the age of fifty—passed the state bar examination and opened his own office.

The elder Newman remained a practicing attorney until his death at the age of eighty-three. So deep was his concern for others that the Mexican government awarded him the Order of the Aztec Eagle for his service to Mexican nationals in the United States. He is one of only a half-dozen non-Mexicans ever to be so honored.

Philip's brother Anthony joined their father's firm five years after it had opened, and then Philip followed in their footsteps by receiving his law degree in 1941.

The Second World War interrupted the start of his career, and it wasn't until 1945—after service with the Coast Guard in the North Pacific—that he, too, was able to join the increasingly respected firm of Newman & Newman—and now there was a third Newman.

He was a trail-blazing lawyer, winning search-and-seizure decisions on behalf of his clients that opened whole new federal interpretations of the law. Others cases won by Philip have caused Congress to improve and amend some of the nation's immigration statutes.

In addition to winning landmark legal cases and writing law books in his spare time, Philip Newman became active in the Mexican-American community, helping found the Community Services Organization, raising money for scholarships, and offering counsel when it was needed. The community responded by naming him CSO Man of the Year.

His talents were recognized in 1964 by Governor Brown, who appointed him to the Municipal bench in Los Angeles, a position which he won by election in 1972 for a six-year term.

The year after his appointment, Judge Newman was invited to a White House Conference on Mexican-American Problems, and the year after that was appointed to the legal-services program of the Office of Economic Opportunity's National Advisory Committee. In 1967 he testified before the cabinet hearings on Mexican-American Problems in El Paso, Texas.

Aware of the problems faced by the nation's Spanish-speaking citizens, and determined that they benefit from the United State's judicial system, Judge Newman also feels strongly that success is a matter of determination and hard work.

"There is success for all of us," he says, "and I disagree with the 'crepe-hangers' who doom-say the death of our culture and stress the negatives in our society.

"It is difficult to start from point zero to reach a goal. But my father proved it could be done then, and it can be done now. The struggle makes better men at the end."

Grace Olivarez

Grace Olivarez

Considering the career of Grace Gil Olivarez, it is difficult to believe she was a high-school dropout. The first woman ever to graduate from the University of Notre Dame's law school, she overcame a shaky start in life and translated a native intelligence and concern for others into years of distinguished public service — and remains deeply involved in the most pressing social problems of this generation.

Currently director of the University of New Mexico Institute for Social Research and Development, Mrs. Olivarez has also served with the Office of Economic Opportunity, the National Urban Coalition, the U.S. Civil Rights Commission, and other agencies committed to providing a better life for all.

Born to a Spanish father and a Mexican-Irish mother in a small mining town near Phoenix, Arizona, Grace spoke only Spanish until her late teens, though she was able to speak English too.

She recalls the conflict between two cultures, in which many young Mexican-Americans are still trapped: "In school in the Southwest you are literally punished physically if you are caught speaking Spanish in the hallways. The argument was that you couldn't learn English if you spoke Spanish. You were taught that you mustn't speak Spanish, yet you went home and your parents said you must speak Spanish because the Mexican heritage is rich."

School was not a rewarding experience for her, and when the family moved to Phoenix when she was sixteen, Grace dropped out of high school. "I panicked when I saw that large campus, so I went to business college instead."

She went to work thereafter but was laid off in the recession of the Korean War. It was the best thing that ever happened to her. She became the first woman disc jockey in Phoenix, and then moved to a Spanish-speaking radio station in the same city, where she rose to women's-program director.

Mrs. Olivarez wrote, produced, and broadcast daily programs that dealt with everything from cooking to social development, and interviewed prominent people in fields ranging from sports to international politics.

Meanwhile, she involved herself in civil-rights programs, and that involvement brought her to the attention of the Reverend Theodore M. Hesburgh, president of Notre Dame. Impressed with her intelligence and concern, he waived the requirements for law-school admission—a high-school diploma and a college degree—and invited Mrs. Olivarez to enroll. She did.

In 1970 she became the first woman graduate of the law school, and that same year was appointed by President Nixon to the Commission on Population Growth and the American Future.

The young girl once frightened by high school emerged as a mature woman with exciting promise. For a year she served as director of Arizona's State Office of Economic Opportunity, and has also been executive secretary for the National Conference on Poverty in the Southwest, a staff specialist for the Choate Foundation of Phoenix, counseling Mexican-American and black families, and a special researcher on the chronically unemployed for the U.S. Department of Labor.

Mrs. Olivarez—divorced and with a young son now—has been on many panels concerned with social betterment, and the awards and honors that have come to her, in themselves, would fill pages.

As director of the Institute for Social Research and Development at the University of New Mexico, Mrs. Olivarez heads a program that operates under more than 2.75 million dollars in contracts and appropriations. The institute is concerned with programs dealing with education, management, social and economic development, technology, leisure, recreation, and criminal justice.

Mrs. Olivarez would like to see New Mexico become the leader in dealing with problems of population, environment, and poverty. And she reminds other Mexican-Americans that no one lives in a vacuum: "No one can go it alone. Somewhere along the way is the person who gives you that job, who has faith that you can make it. And everyone has something to work with, if only he will look for it."

Jim Plunkett

Jim Plunkett

Had the question ever arisen, it is unlikely anyone would have believed that Jim Plunkett—an introspective boy who had suffered a childhood bone disease and later a thyroid tumor—would one day grow up to be possibly the best collegiate quarterback in the nation's history. But he did.

His football talents now already a legend at Stanford University, the strapping six-foot-two, 212-pound Mexican-American won the Heisman Trophy, led his team to a record number of victories during the regular seasons and in the Rose Bowl, and set a new career mark in total offense in the National Collegiate Athletic Association before turning pro.

And his story, in more ways than one, is just beginning.

Plunkett was born to blind parents in San Jose, California, in 1947, the surname coming from an admixture of German-Irish on his father's side. Because of his handicap, the elder Plunkett was forced to support the family (which also included two daughters) on a salary he earned as a news vendor. Jim began helping out as soon as he was old enough to count change—first selling newspapers and then working in a service station.

Until he was a fifth-grader, Plunkett was just a homebody too big for his age, a child without apparent special interests. And then he discovered sports.

He became a schoolboy athletic star almost at once, excelling in basketball, wrestling, track, and baseball, and then discovered a football-passing ability that was far from ordinary.

Football became young Jim's first interest, and he pursued

it with a vigor that came to typify his seasons at Stanford. In his last two years in high school, he led his team to two championships and was named to the All-League team. As a senior he was selected for the North Shrine All-Star team.

Offers of football scholarships came from many universities and colleges when Plunkett was graduated from high school. He chose Stanford for its high academic reputation and the fact that it was near his home. He could be where his parents needed him.

Doctors found a tumor on Plunkett's thyroid just before he entered Stanford. It was benign, but recuperation delayed the patient's entrance into the freshman football lineup, and when he finally did leave the bench, his performance was inadequate.

Later, however, he would make up for the shaky start by never falling below a B average academically and by establishing himself as a football champion of rare measure.

In his first year in the varsity lineup (1968) Plunkett completed 142 out of 268 passes for 2,156 yards and fourteen touchdowns—a record in the Pacific Eight Conference. The price was a few cracked ribs and an injured knee, but they obviously did not detract to any great extent from the brilliant first varsity year.

The following season was even greater for the maturing young star. Plunkett set Pacific Eight records for passing yardage, touchdown passes, total offense yardage, and total offense in a single game. Nationally he ranked fifth in passing and third in total offense.

When his original class graduated without him, Plunkett became technically eligible for the pro draft. His father had died a year before, and the dazzling quarterback—by now a star of nationwide prominence—was tempted to take the money the pros were offering in order to support his mother.

But a single overriding consideration induced him to remain at Stanford for his final year. Plunkett had volunteered over the years to counsel Mexican-American children in career and life guidance, and he asked now: "How could I tell them not to drop out of high school if I dropped out of Stanford?"

He stayed for that last season and led his team to the Pacific Eight championship and victory in the Rose Bowl, at the same time breaking most of his own records. It won him the Heisman Memorial Trophy as the best college football player in America.

Plunkett has since joined the New England Patriots, and the Boston fans have already taken him to their hearts. The young star smiles and says, "Maybe we can build a winner." In more ways than most ever anticipated, he already has.

Luis Quero-Chiesa

Luis Quero-Chiesa

Luis Quero-Chiesa is the modern embodiment of the Renaissance man. Civic and cultural leader, he is an artist, a master calligrapher, fiction writer, essayist, biographer, lecturer, and chairman of the New York City Board of Higher Education. Among other things.

Quero-Chiesa, in fact, is the first Puerto Rican ever appointed to the board, and he has blazed significant trails not only on behalf of young people of Puerto Rican descent but for all the students of the big city.

By virtue of outlook as well as multiplicity of talents, he is not only a Renaissance man but a giant in the social affairs of New York as well.

Born in the stately old city of Ponce, Puerto Rico, in 1911, Quero-Chiesa pursued art at an early age. He studied in Puerto Rico, and then, when he was eighteen, entered the Parsons School of Design in New York, where he was graduated as a specialist in graphic arts and advertising.

But the specialty notwithstanding, young Luis continued painting, and his works have influenced the development of a movement toward a strong Puerto Rican art based on native motifs. His works have won critical acclaim at exhibits in New York and San Juan, and were included in a traveling exhibit of American artists shown throughout the western hemisphere.

Even painting, however, has not alone been enough to satisfy Quero-Chiesa's abundance of creative energy. His essays, short stories, and cultural commentaries have appeared in the leading publications of Latin America, including the *Anthology of Puerto Rican Authors, The General*

Anthology of Puerto Rican Short Stories, and *The Art of the Short Story in Puerto Rico.*

Quero-Chiesa became active in New York's Puerto Rican community the year he entered the city in 1929. Under his leadership, the Institute of Puerto Rico, New York's oldest Puerto Rican cultural organization, has carried out the most extensive cultural program in the history of the community.

He led in the establishment of the Institute of Puerto Rico Cultural Awards and in 1960 founded the Youth Group, a self-governing organization oriented toward cultural programs and antidelinquency activities.

Quero-Chiesa's efforts in New York did not go unnoticed, and in 1965 Mayor Robert Wagner named him to the Board of Higher Education to fill a vacancy caused by death. He was reappointed by Mayor John Lindsay in 1966 for a full nine-year term.

Minority groups in New York City have gained significantly during Quero-Chiesa's tenure on the board. He was responsible in 1969 for the Committee on Expanded Educational Opportunity, a group instrumental in the growth of special programs for minority students, and for steps to liberalize admission standards.

Two special programs established by the Committee on Expanded Educational Opportunity provide money and tutorial services for students with academic deficiencies but college potential. About 3,400 Puerto Rican students are enrolled in the program.

Quero-Chiesa, whose own higher education was gleaned from books in the New York public libraries, has been instrumental also in establishment of new colleges in the city university system, notably La Guardia Community College and Eugenio María de Hostos, which have bilingual programs.

In an observation of his work with the Institute of Puerto Rico, Quero-Chiesa summarized an important element of his own attitude: "While we exalt and propagate the finer aspects of Puerto Rican culture, we do it not with the purpose of isolating the Puerto Ricans in a cultural ghetto, paralyzing them in the very midst of this vibrant, pulsating, creative America, but rather in the belief that the more the Puerto Rican immigrant—or any other immigrant, for that matter— knows about himself and his native culture, the greater and finer his contribution will be to American life."

Luis Quero-Chiesa's contribution, for that and a variety of reasons, has been immense.

Anthony Quinn

Anthony Quinn

Anthony Quinn was born poor and with a speech impediment. Today he owns a villa in Rome, a home in Beverly Hills, and is generally recognized as one of the world's most accomplished actors. The story of how he got there embraces elements of drama almost as compelling as the characters and situations he has created in the movies and on the stage.

It began in Chihuahua, Mexico, in 1915, where Anthony Rudolph Oaxaca Quinn was born to Frank Quinn, an Irishman fighting for Pancho Villa, and Manuela Oaxaca, a Mexican girl of Aztec ancestry.

While the Pancho Villa revolution was in progress, his mother smuggled her small son out of the country into El Paso, Texas. Quinn would recall years later: "It gave me claustrophobia. I was hidden in a wagon under a pile of coal, and I nearly choked to death."

The father joined the family in Texas, and when Tony was four they moved to Los Angeles, where the elder Quinn got a job in a movie studio as a prop man.

Tony sometimes went to work with his father, and once, at a very early age, played the part of a juvenile Tarzan in a jungle movie. It was the unheralded beginning of a career that would come to spectacular fruition years later.

When the boy was only nine, his father was killed in an automobile accident, and Tony had to take part-time jobs to help support himself and his mother. He attended school in Los Angeles, played with other Mexican-American children, and tried his hand at both sculpturing and playing the saxophone.

There was no possibility of a college education in the depression 1930's. Tony, who had been foreman of an apricot ranch at fourteen, worked up and down the West Coast—as a cement mixer, ditch digger, boxer, electrician, butcher, paper salesman, clothes cutter, and foreman in a mattress factory.

The small acting part he had won as a boy had influenced him, but a speech impediment seemed destined to keep him from the stage. But then, when he was nineteen, Tony had the impediment corrected, and less than a year later played the lead in *Clean Beds* for a little-theater group.

Two more plays followed, one of them Noel Coward's *Hay Fever*. "Imagine," Quinn says now, "a lower-class Mexican kid from the east side of L.A. doing a sophisticated English comedy!"

He began his film career at the age of twenty-one with *The Plainsman,* and over the years has portrayed a dancing, shouting, *living Zorba the Greek,* the meditative French painter Paul Gauguin in *Lust for Life,* the Arab chieftain in *Lawrence of Arabia,* the Russian Pope in *The Shoes of the Fisherman,* and the used-up boxer in *Requiem for a Heavyweight.*

He received his first Academy Award as best supporting actor in 1952 for his portrayal of a Mexican killer in *Viva Zapata!* In 1956 he won another Oscar for best supporting actor in *Lust for Life.* The Italian movie *La Strada,* in which Quinn played the role of a brutish circus strongman, was named the best foreign-language movie of the year, also in 1956.

Quinn—who has appeared in 106 films—worked hard at the business of acting. He took any role offered him at first, and even as a major star throws himself into the creation of the roles he plays. He insists on "becoming" each character he portrays, and constantly seeks self-improvement and self-evaluation.

In explanation of the extraordinary amount of effort he puts into his roles, Quinn says, "No one who has ever gone hungry can escape the fear of going hungry again."

His stage career has included *The Gentleman from Athens* and the touring company of *A Streetcar Named Desire* early in his career, and later *Becket* and *Tchin-Tchin.* He has also written an autobiography, *The Original Sin.*

Once asked why he acted, the famed Mexican-American star replied, "I am looking for a sense of order. I imagined a better world than I've found. When I was a kid I had illusions about what the world should be, and a sense of beauty that has not been verified by my experience.

"I act because I envision a better world than the one that exists."

José Quintero

José Quintero

Until he saw Bette Davis in a movie, José Quintero felt that he might someday enter the priesthood. It was one of those moments in a young man's life when, by accident, he stumbles over his destiny, and nothing is the same for him thereafter. That's how it happened to Quintero. A chance movie altered the course of his future and brought him from Panama into the world of the New York stage.

Born in Panama City in 1924, the son of a Spanish cattle rancher, brewer, and politician, young José attended La Salle Catholic High School. He undertook a course of study that was leading toward the priesthood until he saw that Bette Davis movie.

He abandoned any   of the clergy then and decided that his future lay in acting. He saw all of Miss Davis' movies, and upon graduation from high school persuaded his father to send him to college in Los Angeles, where Hollywood was the capital of the movie industry.

Quintero admits that academically his two years at Los Angeles City College were not productive. But it was in Los Angeles that he saw his first play, *Life with Father*. At the time, however, he spoke Spanish and only very little English, and except for feeling uneasy over slangy use of the word "God," the acting was lost on him.

Later, however, as his mastery of English improved, he saw *The Corn Is Green* and liked it so well that he returned to see it for every night of its two-week run.

The impact of the stage on Quintero's life was immediately obvious. He transferred to the University of Southern California and began studying drama. After receiving his bachelor's degree, Quintero persuaded his father (who had hoped his son would study medicine) to pay his way through the Goodman Theatre Dramatic School in Chicago.

At Goodman he met the young actress Geraldine Page, later to become a first lady of the theater. They would meet again someday, and Quintero would help propel her to stardom.

In the summer of 1949, Quintero and a few other drama students decided it was time to strike out on their own. They headed east and established a summer theater at Woodstock, New York, where the youth who had been determined until then to be an actor suddenly discovered he liked directing better.

Quintero directed *The Glass Menagerie* and *Riders to the Sea,* and by the end of the summer the group had gained profit enough to impel them to remain in New York as the Loft Players. Their first play was *Dark of the Moon* in 1951, and it won four awards for off-Broadway theater.

The following year, one of their productions was *Summer and Smoke* in which Geraldine Page starred. The critics lavished praise on both Miss Page for her acting and Quintero for his directing. Over the years, it has rarely diminished for either.

Many other plays followed, including their first original play, *The Lonely Steeple.*

Even when the critics have been harsh on Quintero, they have tempered their words with praise. Wrote *The New York Times*: "As a director, José Quintero has two mannerisms that are disillusioning. In the climactic moments he sets his actors shouting in a harsh frenzy that his little theater can hardly contain. Quintero is also overfond of silences. But those are his trademarks, and they should not divert attention from the fact that he also has insight into a script and a gift for organizing a performance."

Quintero, who has achieved the kind of reputation that allows a man to talk back to critics, shrugs. "I do not like fast-paced shows," he says. "I prefer subtlety and atmosphere. And particularly silences. Silence is as eloquent as words. Characters without some silences tend to be too secure, just people mechanically reciting lines."

Dr. Henry M. Ramírez

Dr. Henry M. Ramírez

In the days before social activism had become an American catch phrase, Henry Ramírez was a social activist. He ꜱꜰꜰ.ₜₑ a program in the 1950's called New Horizons to motivate young chicano toughs, the "vatos locos," toward education as a springboard to a better life. For as a onetime teen-age tough himself, a "pachuco" in the 1940's, he knew what a difference it could make.

Dr. Henry M. Ramírez, chairman of the Cabinet Committee on Opportunities for Spanish-Speaking People, was born in Walnut, California, the son of migratory farm workers. He was raised in the barrios of Pomona and, along with ten brothers and sisters, became a migrant worker himself so the family could survive.

Ramírez's parents had fled the turmoil of post-revolution Mexico and had come to the United States in the depression years. His father was an electrician but could find work only as a railroad laborer. An injury caused his dismissal from that job, and they became migrant farm workers.

During his youth, the family felt the sting of racial humiliations, and Henry in defense joined other Mexican-Americans in "pachuco" gangs. "I don't know how many kids today can recall not being allowed to swim in a public pool or being refused service in a restaurant," he says. "I can."

But education saved Ramírez from the unpleasant alternative of street fighting. A bright and willing student, he at first studied for the priesthood in a Catholic seminary, but left because "I felt I could help my people more on the outside." From there it was on to a Ph.D. from Loyola University.

It was as a language teacher at Whittier High School that Dr. Ramírez established the New Horizons program to get the "vatos locos," the crazy guys, off the streets and into the classrooms. The program is still in existence.

Summoned to Washington, D.C., in 1968, he became director of the Mexican-American Studies Division for the U.S. Commission on Civil Rights. Then, in 1971, President Nixon named him chairman of the Cabinet Committee on Opportunities for Spanish-Speaking People.

Typically, Dr. Ramírez took on the new responsibility with vigor and faced the problem squarely: "The only reason the Spanish-Speaking community needs the committee is because we are not woven into the fabric of government. We have not been 'dealt in' on the power-structure end of decision-making in America."

He called for more involvement by the Spanish-speaking people in government and society as a whole, to "get their share of the good life." At the same time, Dr. Ramírez believes the job of the Cabinet Committee is to create in Washington an understanding of and a sensitivity to the problems of the nation's twelve million Spanish-speaking people.

Having demonstrated by early social activism that his concern was not fad-oriented, he urged the young particularly to have patience with the system which is finally working on behalf of the minority communities. "It is working slowly," he said, "but it *is* working."

As for the turmoil in the barrios, Dr. Ramírez insisted that even that is a sign of progress.

"We are getting closer to our goal, and that is why the people are getting impatient. Kids today are starting to make it through high school, while in my day they were lucky to get through junior high."

And now the onetime migrant worker and street tough has been given the opportunity to move the nation even closer to the goal of equal opportunity.

"The Fourteenth Amendment is there to provide equal opportunities to all members of society, but up to now the Fourteenth Amendment has meant merely the documentation of violations—we're moving now toward implementing the law, and it's a beautiful concept."

Anthony Ríos

youth sometimes acts with impatience. They simply have to learn, he says, about "the long, slow process of building barrio power and learning how to use it."

Geraldo Rivera

Geraldo Rivera

When Geraldo Rivera at twenty-eight was named the top television newsman in New York, the state's Associated Press Broadcasters Association called him "a special kind of individualist in a medium which too often breeds plastic newsmen." The description is perfect.

Rivera is indeed individualistic, and it is the kind of passionate individualism that finds him deeply involved not only with fellow Puerto Ricans in New York but also with all who are struggling to survive. "I make no pretense of objectivity," he says. "I'm in the business of change."

The man whom *Newsweek* magazine describes as "one of the hottest young television reporters in the country" was a child of poverty. Born in Manhattan and raised in a Puerto Rican "enclave" in Brooklyn, Rivera attended public schools in New York.

After high school he sailed with the merchant marine, then bummed around the Southwest before entering the University of Arizona, where he received his B.S. Later he graduated from Brooklyn Law School, was a Smith fellow at the University of Pennsylvania, and then was admitted to the New York bar.

As an attorney, Rivera plunged into the problem of human rights. He was active in the Legal Service Program of the Office of Economic Opportunity, Community Action for Legal Services, the Harlem Assertion of Rights Neighborhood Law Office, and the Black and Brown Caucus.

It was just about the time that Rivera had decided "it was

impossible for me to change the destinies of anyone as a
poverty lawyer" when television beckoned. Rivera heard from
a friend that New York's WABC was looking for a bilingual
reporter. He got the job.

That was in June 1970. Since then, Rivera—who insists
that his first name Geraldo be given the Spanish pronuncia-
tion of Hair-AHL-doe—has won seventy awards and the reputation of a crusading journalist in one of the world's major
cities.

A three-part special report called *Drug Crisis in East Harlem* included a segment filmed in a tenement next door to his
own home on the Lower East Side. It was this show that won
Rivera the AP Award and distinction as an individualistic
reporter.

But there was even greater acclaim for his ten-part series
Willowbrook: The Last Great Disgrace—a searching docu-
mentary exposing the abominable conditions at the Willowbrook State School for the Mentally Retarded on Staten
Island.

He showed scenes of children in bare rooms festering in
their own feces and moaning incomprehensibly, and told the
television audience: "This is what it looked like. This is what
it sounded like. But how can I tell you about the way it
smelled?"

The series won him fifteen awards and prompted Governor
Rockefeller to restore twenty million dollars that had been
previously cut from the Willowbrook budget.

Rivera's philosophy of journalism is deceptively simple.
"I report the news as I see it," he says. "The tragedy and
humor of people who live in New York City, a place so un-
civilized that survival really means staying alive. Sometimes
people don't want to see the kind of stories I report on because they're sad or ugly. But they happen just a stone's throw
away."

His own success, the handsome Rivera says, is similarly a
success for the Puerto Rican community. New Yorkers can
see that the stereotype of the Puerto Rican as a threat to their
safety is nonsense.

He remains involved, meanwhile, in the activities of his
community and continues on the Puerto Rican Legal Defense
Fund, the New York Board of Corrections, and the New York
Urban Coalition.

Outstanding television reporter and author of a book on the

Willowbrook situation and two children's books, Rivera confided to a friend once that his ultimate ambition was to become mayor of New York.

Few doubt that if he really wants it, he'll get it.

Ambassador Horacio Rivero

Ambassador Horacio Rivero

When a man involves himself in a career that spans almost half a century and rises to the very top of his profession over formidable competition, one would presume that upon his retirement at age sixty-two he would turn at last to the easy life. But such presumptions must reckon with the man in question. And Horacio Rivero is not ready to rest.

An admiral in the Navy, a highly decorated blue-water sailor as well as a distinguished Pentagon planner, Rivero retired from the military service in 1972, but not from the service of his country.

Shortly after he ended one career, he was appointed by President Nixon as United States ambassador to Spain—the first person of Spanish descent ever to represent this country in Spain. And a new career was beginning.

Horacio Rivero, once described as "the minority no one knows," was born in 1910 in Ponce, Puerto Rico. He was graduated from Central High School in San Juan and entered the U.S. Naval Academy at Annapolis in 1927.

Rivero was an outstanding cadet, and four years later was commissioned an ensign, ranking academically third in a class of 441. By July 1949 he was a captain, by 1956 a rear admiral, by 1962 a vice-admiral, and by 1964 a full admiral.

Rivero served aboard many vessels as gunnery officer and communications officer in the years following Annapolis, until 1938, when he attended Naval Postgraduate School and the Massachusetts Institute of Technology, where he received a Master of Science degree in electrical engineering.

When the Second World War broke out, Rivero was as-

signed as assistant gunnery officer aboard the USS *San Juan*
and participated in the landings at Guadalcanal, in raids on
the Gilbert Islands, and in the Battle of Santa Cruz Islands.

For his conduct during all three encounters, he was
awarded the Bronze Star with Combat "V" for meritorious
service.

Rivero served on the *San Juan* for most of the war, but near
the end became executive officer of the USS *Pittsburgh,*
taking part in the Okinawa and Iwo Jima campaigns and in
the first carrier raids on Tokyo.

The big ship was caught in a typhoon near Japan and lost
part of her bow in the storm. But because of Rivero's actions,
the crew brought the *Pittsburgh* into port under her own
steam. He was again cited, this time with the Legion of Merit
for risking his life for the safety of his men and the preserva-
tion of his ship.

Detached from the *Pittsburgh* after the war, Rivero served
as assistant for special weapons in the Office of Naval Operations, where he was awarded the Navy Commendation Medal,
this time demonstrating his talents on an administrative level.
He also participated on the staffs of task forces during atomic
tests at Bikini and Eniwetok.

After a short tour as commander of the destroyer *William
Lawe,* Rivero—by then captain—was summoned to the
Pentagon as one of the original members of the Weapons
System Evaluation Group.

Later he attended courses at the National War College and
became assistant chief of staff for the vast Pacific Fleet. A
year later Rivero became a rear admiral and was named deputy chief of Armed Forces Special Weapons and later director of the Long Range Objectives Group, Office of the
Chief of Naval Operations.

In 1962 Rivero was promoted to vice-admiral and named
commander of the Amphibious Force for the entire Atlantic
Fleet, and simultaneously won a gold star in lieu of his second
Legion of Merit for exceptionally meritorious conduct. The
citation read in part: "During the Cuban crisis he assured the
readiness of the Atlantic Fleet Amphibious Forces to react
swiftly and decisively at any time and place required."

Admiral Rivero—who has held a variety of other positions—rose to commander in chief of the Allied Forces in
southern Europe in 1964, and was decorated many more times
before his retirement in 1972. With the beginning of a new

career as U.S. ambassador to Spain, "the minority no one
knows" may become one of the best-known in contemporary
America.

Juan "Chi Chi" Rodríguez

Juan "Chi Chi" Rodríguez

Juan "Chi Chi" Rodríguez was born twice—once in 1935 on a plantation in Puerto Rico and once in 1972 on a golf course in Dallas, Texas. The first time was real, the second time symbolic, but don't tell Chi Chi that the second wasn't as important as the first. He knows better. The maturation process represented by the rebirth brought him $112,000 that year.

A small man (five-seven, 135 pounds) with a big swing (300 yards), Rodriguez loved golf from the beginning. His father was a poor plantation worker, and Chi Chi—a name he adopted from a baseball player who was his childhood idol—began caddying at age six to supplement the family income.

He recalls those days with mixed feelings. He was near his favorite game, and often, after working hours, practiced at it by hitting tin cans along the street with a club fashioned from a guava tree. But at the same time, he despairs of a childhood filled with work and in later years would often say, "I love children because I was never one myself. I was too poor."

Rodríguez boxed and played baseball in high school, but dropped out in the eleventh grade, again for overriding financial reasons. Three years later he competed against golf professionals for the first time, without much success, and that same year joined the Army for a two-year hitch.

It was after he was discharged from the service that the golfer Chi Chi truly began to emerge. He became assistant to the pro at El Dorado Beach Hotel in Puerto Rico and worked hard at perfecting a swing that was startlingly powerful.

In 1960 Chi Chi brought home his first purse. Using women's clubs because they are lighter, he played in twelve tournaments, finished fourth in one, and won $2,262. Three years later—developing what he calls a "solid-wall stance"—he won his first PGA title, the Denver Open, and what seemed a whopping $17,674 for the year.

The following year, 1964, Rodríguez won two major tournaments, took second in two others, and established himself at last as a force to be reckoned with in the highly competitive world of professional golf. His earnings that memorable year were $48,338.

He was riding high, clowning often to please the crowds, doffing his hat to a band of admirers that called themselves "Chi Chi's Bandidos," donating money to worthy causes, and winning fat purses. The high life continued for a while. Then something happened.

Chi Chi himself admits that there were a couple of dry years. At the end of 1971 he looked back on earlier triumphs and tried to determine what important element of victory he had lost—what magic. His earnings had tapered off, his jokes didn't seem as funny, and he was in less than top condition.

There were long runs and daily jogging on the beaches, regular exercise periods, and a steady hardening of the flab. Additionally, there was an important decision for the fun-loving Chi Chi: from now on he would banter with the customers *after* the birdie putt, not before.

That precipitated the rebirth in 1972, a year that won him the Byron Nelson Classic in Dallas, plus some seconds and thirds in other tourneys. His total was impressive: in all ten contests, he finished in the top ten.

From 1963 to 1972, the powerful, diminutive Chi Chi won half a million dollars.

Is he happy? Never happier. In addition to his earnings, Rodríguez is doing the thing he likes most, and meeting people at that. He explains his luck tersely. "I love people." And people, the years have shown, love Chi Chi.

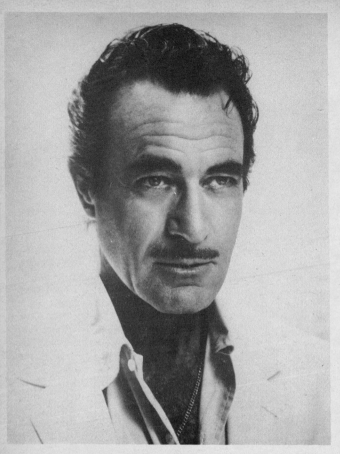

Gilbert Roland

Gilbert Roland

No one ever belittled the Cisco Kid. There were two reasons for that. First, the Kid—among the more memorable of movie heroes—just wasn't the kind of hombre you pushed around. Secondly, and more importantly, the man who portrayed the swashbuckling Kid refused to participate in any role that would denigrate either Mexico or Mexican-Americans.

Gilbert Roland, a screen star since 1927, going back into the era of silent films, is even more serious now about not accepting parts that tend to downgrade his people. He remains active in movie and television work and insists on fighting the insensitivities of the entertainment industry in its characterization of Mexican-Americans.

"When I look at some of the movies, TV shows, and commercials portraying Mexicans like payasos [clowns] I say to myself, 'There goes more misunderstanding because some writer or producer was too lazy to learn his subject matter.'"

Gilbert Roland was born Luis Alonso in Ciudad Juarez, Chihuahua, Mexico. His parents were emigrants from Spain, where his father and grandfather had been bullfighters. Even in Mexico, Roland's father owned a bull ring, and the boy took his first job there at age eight, sharpening swords, selling cushions, and dreaming of the day he too would fight bulls.

The Alonso family fled to Texas before Pancho Villa, and when he was but fourteen Roland left El Paso and hopped a freight train to Hollywood. "I went there," he would recall later, "to be a movie star. Life wasn't so pretty for me as a kid. Motion pictures were my whole existence. I fell in love with the people on the screen."

Though he had only $2.60 in his pocket, Roland made it to southern California and got a job as a movie extra. He copied his screen name after his two favorite movie stars, John Gilbert and Ruth Roland, and threw himself into his work.

For a few years Roland had bit parts, and then won the role of Armand Duval opposite Norma Talmadge in *Camille.* That was in 1933. Since then, the actor's career has risen steadily, interrupted only by his work in Air Force intelligence during the Second World War.

Roland has played in *The Big Circus, Around the World in Eighty Days, Beneath the Twelve Mile Reef,* and many other films. But the role most associated with Roland is the part he played as the glamorous Cisco Kid, a kind of Mexicanized Robin Hood.

Even in the days preceding the wave of racial awareness in the United States, Roland was insisting that the portrayal of chicanos be treated with respect. He recalls once asking that a piece of dialogue be altered to show the Kid reading Shakespeare by a river bank.

"I wanted to be sure the Mexican was not portrayed as an unwashed, uneducated savage clown," Roland would say. "I refuse roles that picture Mexicans as ridiculous, quaint, or foolish."

Roland adds that he never joined any chicano media group, even though he has fought to improve the image of the Mexican-American in films and on television. He has gone to California's Washington legislators in person to ask for bilingual education in the barrios and for other benefits to improve the lot of Mexican-Americans.

"I am an individualist," he explains, "and must get things accomplished in my own way."

Roland, who became a U.S. citizen in 1942, is also a talented writer. He won a *Writer's Digest* story contest with a piece called "A Glass of Wine," and two of his short stories have been published in *Toros* magazine. He also wrote a script for television.

The actor-writer produced one screenplay, called "the first honest story of the Mexican revolution, with Mexicans as they are—warm, genuine, without pretense,"

Rubén Salazar

Eulogies are often exaggerated measures of a person's life, but when an editorial writer observed that "Rubén Salazar was a most uncommon man," the measure was accurate. Salazar was an exceptional newspaper reporter and columnist, a talented television executive, and an eloquent exponent of the Mexican-American cause. Even in death his impact lingers on.

Salazar died on the forward fringe of the movement to uplift the standard of his people. He was, characteristically, in the middle of the story when a tear-gas projectile struck him dead in the barrio of East Los Angeles on August 29, 1970. He had almost predicted the tragedy a few days earlier, when, encouraged by progress in the area of human rights, he commented to a friend, "Everything is going so well that something just has to go wrong."

Rubén Salazar was born in Chihuahua, Mexico, on March 3, 1928. His family moved to the United States when he was still an infant, and he was raised in El Paso, where he eventually received a Bachelor of Arts degree at the University of Texas.

After a two-year hitch in the Army (and the attainment of his U.S. citizenship), Salazar went to work for the El Paso *Herald-Post* and plunged deeply into investigative reporting— turning up stories on jail conditions and drug abuse. A short while later he moved to California and the Santa Rosa *Press-Democrat,* then the *San Francisco News,* the Los Angeles *Herald-Express,* and finally, the *Los Angeles Times* in 1959.

It was at the prestigious *Times* that the talented and innovative Salazar achieved his greatest success. He worked in the city room of the big newspaper, covered the war in Vietnam, wrote of revolutionary foment in Latin America, and was a member of the *Times'* bureau in Mexico City for two years before returning to Los Angeles as a specialist in Mexican-American affairs.

A precise and objective reporter, Salazar eventually became a prize-winning columnist for the newspaper, and simultaneously was appointed news director for KMEX-TV, a growing and influential Spanish-language television station in Los Angeles.

As a commentator in print and on the air, he consistently spoke out on behalf of the Mexican-American community, angered that the pride of his people had been "dragged through the mud of racism since the Anglos arrived in the Southwest."

He called for a shakeup in the Establishment "so that it will include us in," and warned that the inequities of the system were encouraging militancy among the chicanos.

While his journalistic career often thrust Salazar into the center of turmoil, he was fundamentally a man of peace, and the violence of his death is a study in irony.

It was a day of protest for the National Chicano Moratorium Committee which had organized a march in East Los Angeles against the war in Vietnam. Salazar, on the scene to cover the event for his column in the *Times* and for KMEX-TV, was seated in a café. Somehow, trouble began in the streets. A tear-gas projectile was fired. And Rubén Salazar—a man who had dodged gunfire around the world—lay dead at age forty-two on the floor of an American café.

Expressions of grief came from across the nation—from the White House and from the barrios, where the name Salazar had made such impact. Newspapers in Mexico bannered the story on page one, that a hero of social change in the United States had fallen.

There were cries of outrage along with grief, and demands for investigations to fix the blame. A close friend would remark later, "Injustice is to blame. Violence is to blame. Whoever causes either is to blame."

Honors and praise came to the dead journalist, for the words he had written and for the movement he had come to represent in southern California. A park was renamed in his honor in East Los Angeles.

But what would have mattered more to him is that the fight to eradicate racism goes on, and the name Rubén Salazar is mentioned often.

Ambassador Phillip Sánchez

Ambassador Phillip Sánchez

From California crop-picker to selection as the highest rank-ing Mexican-American in the administration of President Richard Nixon is a long jump, but Phillip Sánchez made it without being anyone's "house Mexican." He's proud of that.

Once the youngest county executive in California, Sánchez was only forty-one when he was named national director of the Office of Economic Opportunity. Cries of political tokenism—quieted eventually by the man's expertise as head of the OEO—were answered immediately by the Fresno *Bee*.

The newspaper wrote: "Nobody who has observed Sánchez through his years as Fresno County administrative officer would believe he would allow himself to be put on display for anyone's ulterior purposes."

The parents of Phillip Sánchez migrated from Mexico to California in the 1920's, and along with other Mexican-Americans, built a new community called Pinedale, ten miles from Fresno. It was here that Phillip was born, one of seven children.

The father abandoned the family in the depression 1930's, leaving Mrs. Sánchez and her family to travel the San Joaquin Valley as pickers of plums, apricots, grapes, figs, cotton, onions, and potatoes. Phillip was only six, but he worked right along with everybody else.

The family returned to Pinedale at the end of every season in time for the children to attend school in the same system. School was a positive experience for young Phillip. He skipped the third grade, and in the seventh grade passed a test that would have allowed him to pass directly into high school, but his mother decided against it.

Sánchez was one of relatively few Mexican-Americans in the community to attend secondary school. Only he, of the seven children in the family, finished school. He went on from there to Coalinga College, and then, on a scholarship, to Fresno State College, where he was named the outstanding male graduate in his class. That was in 1953, when he received his Bachelor of Arts degree.

Within four years Sánchez was working as an administrative analyst for the state of California in the Fresno County government, and began to display the principles for which he would become so widely known.

One demonstration involved the effort of a gambling syndicate to get Pinedale incorporated and its City Council established—in return for exclusive gambling rights in the city under the state's local-option law.

Sánchez, incensed at the blatant takeover attempt ("It was," he said, "like the plot of a B-movie"), fought the syndicate with petitions and in court to such an extent that the people of Pinedale voted down incorporation—and gambling with it.

Not too many years later, in 1962, the Fresno County Board of Supervisors asked Sánchez to become the county's administrative officer at age thirty-two. At a time when Mexican-Americans were equated with migrant labor, it was a special tribute to his ability and individualism.

That same year, as the youngest county executive in California, Sánchez was named Fresno's Outstanding Young Man, and a year later the state's Jaycees named him one of California's five outstanding young men.

He was also appointed to the California State College Board of Trustees, and was a member of the governing board of the California Community Colleges and the Fresno State College Advisory Board. Additionally, he became deeply involved in charitable affairs and the Mexican-American community.

Then, in 1971, President Nixon asked Sánchez to become assistant director of operations for the Office of Economic Opportunity. A few months later, he became its director.

Thus he became the first Mexican-American to head the federal poverty agency, and the highest-ranking Spanish-speaking appointee in the Nixon administration, a post he held until 1973, when he was named ambassador to Honduras.

Raymond Télles

Raymond Télles

Raymond Télles is the kind of man about whom people wonder: What will he do next? A civil servant under five presidents of the United States, a former politician, civic leader, diplomat, and Air Force colonel, he became a member of the Equal Employment Opportunity Commission in 1971, and there is every indication that his active career still has a long way to go.

A native of El Paso, Texas, Télles entered public service in 1934 as a government accountant and stayed until the outbreak of the Second World War, when he joined the Air Force. Later he would also serve in Korea, where he rose to the rank of colonel.

Télles' subsequent career in the foreign service was enhanced during the Second World War when for three years he was responsible for a program that furnished aircraft and equipment to all of Latin America. He was also liaison officer with the Mexican Air Force. After the war he served as an aide to presidents Truman and Eisenhower on their visits to Mexico City.

Out of uniform in 1947, Télles ran for and was elected to the position of El Paso county clerk in Texas, which he held for four terms. And then he was elected to two terms as mayor of the city of El Paso.

It was on completion of his second term as mayor in 1961 that Télles was appointed United States ambassador to Costa Rica, and was instrumental in that government's acceptance of the Central American Common Market.

He served the U.S. Foreign Service with distinction for six years, but at the end of his tour Washington was not about to relinquish so notable a public servant, and in 1967 he began a two-year ambassadorship to the United States–Mexico Commission for Border Development.

As U.S. chairman of the commission, Télles was responsible to the President for the economic and social development of our border cities with Mexico and for development of friendly relations with the Mexican government and communities.

When the term expired in 1969, Télles became a consultant for private industries. The interlude between government jobs was brief. In 1971 President Nixon appointed him to the Equal Employment Opportunity Commission for a five-year term.

A former student at the University of Texas and a graduate of the International Business College, Télles has received many honors during his long and active career in government service.

Among them have been decorations from the governments of Mexico, Brazil, Peru, Colombia, and Nicaragua.

He was also awarded the Bronze Star by the U.S. Army for bravery in Korea.

Télles and his wife, Delfina, have been honored guests at the inauguration of both presidents Lopez Mateos and Alemán of Mexico, a direct indication of their respect for his statesmanship.

He has also served as United States aid to high dignitaries from Latin America visiting this country.

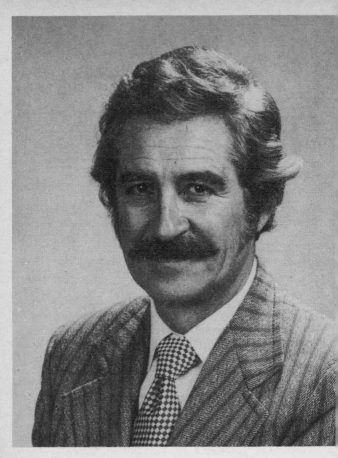

Judge Carlos Terán

Judge Carlos Terán

Carlos Terán's interest in youth is far more than judicial. While he has dealt with their problems as a Superior Court judge of the Juvenile Division, his concern for their well-being has not ended there. Beyond the necessary structured discipline of the courtroom, the man Terán has proved he is as concerned for the welfare of the young as the judge Terán.

As a result, he has taken time to participate in youth-oriented activities on a local level, and has served on state and national committees dedicated to improving the lot of America's children.

Carolos Mendoza Terán was born in 1915 in El Paso, Texas but has been a resident of Los Angeles since he was four.

He attended local schools and then UCLA until the start of the Second World War, when he entered the Army as a private.

Terán won the Bronze Star for bravery under fire as a lieutenant in Italy and was discharged after the war with the rank of captain. He still holds the rank of colonel in the Air Force Reserve.

With the war's end, Terán completed the three-year law course at the University of Southern California and received his Juris Doctor degree in 1949. He was admitted to the California state bar that same year. While practicing law, he took courses at USC which enabled him to receive his Bachelor of Arts degree in 1953.

Terán practiced general law for eight years, when his legal talents were recognized by Governor Goodwin Knight, who appointed him to the Municipal Court in the largely Mexican-

American area of East Los Angeles. Two years later Governor Edmund Brown elevated him to the Superior Court bench.

After becoming a judge, he completed a course of studies at Claremont Graduate School and obtained a master's degree in Government in 1966.

Judge Terán presided in the Juvenile Division about the time his outside work with youth was proliferating to a great degree.

He became active with the Eastside Boys' Club and was named a member of the board of directors of Pitzer College.

Judge Terán was appointed a member of the board of directors of the Boys' Clubs of America in October 1970, and the following year was awarded the Silver Keystone Award for outstanding service to youth, the highest honor accorded by the national organization of Boys' Clubs.

Additionally, Judge Terán has been a delegate to the White House Conference on Children and Youth, and was a member of the Governor's Advisory Committee on Children and Youth for many years.

But as much work as he has done on behalf of youth, the busy jurist has also found time for community activities on an even broader scale.

He has been a member of the board of United Way, the Los Angeles version of coordinated charities; president of the Welfare Planning Council in East-Central Los Angeles; president of the board of the Council of Mexican-American Affairs; president of the Belvedere Coordinating Council; co-chairman of the Citizens Committee for Rapid Transit in Los Angeles; treasurer of the East Los Angeles Bar Association; and an officer in the Mexican Chamber of Commerce in Los Angeles.

Judge Terán also lives an active family life, and has three children of his own.

Ralph de Toledano

Ralph de Toledano

Few who have ever read his books or columns, or who have heard his commentaries on radio and television, remain neutral about Ralph de Toledano. Outspokenly conservative, he has aroused the wrath of moderates and liberals alike, and has been charged by some critics with helping muddy the already dark waters of American politics during the 1950's and 1960's.

Nevertheless, Toledano has also held journalistic editorial positions with *Newsweek* and other responsible journals that demanded objective observation of the affairs of government and of the nation generally. William Buckley has praised him as "among the most talented writers in the world." And, political tendencies notwithstanding, he is also a jazz expert of note and an accomplished poet.

Toledano has written of himself: "I have been called in print a John Bircher, a Communist, and other names. If I must be classified, it must be as a nonconformist conservative with general (though often critical) Republican sympathies. I derive my politics from a belief in God and the dignity of man."

Born of American parents in the International Zone of Tangier in 1916, Toledano turned to writing in high school, where he edited the school magazine *Inklings* and helped found an independent weekly with one thousand subscribers, *Crosstown.*

He pursued his interest at Columbia College, winning awards for both prose and poetry. After receiving his bachelor's degree, Toledano worked first as general editor for what he termed "a string of rather dubious publications" then became an editor of the·*New Leader,* a liberal weekly newspaper with anti-Communist leanings. At the same time he contributed music critiques to the *American Mercury.*

Of Spanish descent, and fluent in both Spanish and French, the journalist entered the Army in the Second World War and was eventually assigned to the Office of Strategic Services and sent to Cornell University for an intensive course in Italian. He was dropped from a projected mission in Italy, however, for being too anti-Communist, and spent the remainder of his Army career in Puerto Rico.

In 1946, at the end of his military career, Toledano returned to New York, where he took over the editorship of a publication produced by a federation of education and religious societies, and then managership of an anti-Communist monthly. For a short period after that, he was publicity director for a labor union.

There followed in 1948 his first major recognition on a national scale when he joined *Newsweek* for twelve years. As an assistant editor, he covered national affairs from New York and then was promoted to national-reports editor, where his reputation as a keen political analyst grew.

Over the years Toledano has covered some of the nation's most important news events, both in and out of politics, and has written fourteen books, among them *Seeds of Treason, Spies, Dupes and Diplomats, Day of Reckoning, Nixon,* and *Lament for a Generation.*

The books received mixed reviews, one being called "a form of poisonous name-dropping" and another being praised as carrying "a greater impact of reality than all the official reports put together."

From *Newsweek* Toledano went on to join the Taft Broadcasting Company as a radio-TV commentator from Washington, and he also joined King Features as a syndicated columnist. Later he switched to National News Research Syndicate. His 750-word essays appear three days a week in newspapers throughout the nation.

In between writing books and columns, the prolific journalist has also managed to publish articles, poetry, and music critiques in such reputable publications as *Reader's Digest, American Scholar, National Review,* and *Modern Age.*

Toledano has made hundreds of speaking appearances and has been honored both by the Veterans of Foreign Wars' and by the Freedoms Foundation.

Lee Treviño

Lee Treviño

Lee Treviño, the amazing "Super Mex" who expanded golf into a sport all could identify with, told reporters once, "Every day when I wake up it's a brand-new day and a brand-new world." The philosophy has carried him far through life, from the limits of despair to the heights of achievement, but the essential Treviño remains unchanged. Even at the dazzling apex of his career, he is still taking life one day at a time for each new world it brings.

On top of the golf kingdom after sweeping three international titles in a month (the U.S., British, and Canadian championships), then following that with his second consecutive win of the British Open. Treviño can still remember a time when life was not all that good. Only hard work and incredible determination lifted him from a shack without electricity or plumbing to a day of victory in 1968.

Lee Buck Treviño was born on December 1, 1939, on the outskirts of Dallas. The maintenance shack where he and two sisters were raised by their mother and immigrant grandfather sat in a hayfield next to a golf course that was to shape the boy's life.

By the time he was six, Treviño was emulating the golfers on the other side of the fence, using horse apples and a five iron he had found and cut down to size. "It was a lonely life," he says. "I was never around anybody. I was all by myself."

His mother worked as a domestic and his grandfather as a gravedigger, but their wages were too low to support the family, So Treviño quite school after the seventh grade and took a job as an assistant greenskeeper at the golf club on the other side of the fence. At the age of fifteen he played his first full eighteen holes and shot a remarkable seventy-seven.

Golf was becoming more and more an integral part of his life. Even in the Marine Corps, which he joined two years later, the sport was an important factor. When he left the service in 1961, Lee returned to Dallas with but one thought—to play golf.

He went to work as a pro at Hardy's Pitch-N-Putt and soon established a reputation as a hard worker, a potentially great golfer, and something of a swinger—the beer-drinking kind.

He played eighteen holes of golf almost every day, worked at Hardy's every day, hit about a thousand balls nearly every day, and still had energy left for night life.

Then he won the Texas Open. And placed second in the Mexican Open. And won the Texas Open again.

Now they were beginning to notice the flashy champ who called himself Super Mex and kept everyone laughing. The name Treviño was spreading, and when he took fifth place in the U.S. Open for 1967 for the six-thousand-dollar purse, the golf world really sat up.

But the following year was Lee's big one, the beginning. By then he had decided to quit his job as a pro and tour with the tournament players. It paid off.

On June 16, 1968, Treviño tied Jack Nicklaus' all-time low-scoring record to win the U.S. Open championship—and thirty thousand dollars. Asked what he'd do with the money, the exalted winner shouted, "I'm going to buy the Alamo and give it back to Mexico!"

Later that year he won the Hawaiian Open, and the following year the Tucson Open and the World Cup championship in Singapore—and tournament after tournament after tournament, including those three big ones in one month in 1971.

Treviño's income is considerable, but the champ's generosity is well known—scholarship funds, personal donations of cash to the poor and the ill, and help in establishing a children's hospital in Memphis and an orphans' home in England.

Nor has he forgotten what golf and his fans (Lee's Fleas, they call themselves) have done for him: "They've been good to me. It's real easy for me to remember just a few years ago when I was a fat little Mexican trying to hustle bets and didn't have two bucks to cover them."

Said *Sports Illustrated* of Treviño, while naming him 1971

Sportsman of the Year: "What Lee Treviño has done is take the game out of the country-club boardroom and put it in the parking lot where everybody can get at it."

Daniel Villanueva

Daniel Villanueva

In a personal-data questionnaire filled out by Daniel Villanueva, the question was asked: "What was the most memorable experience of your life?" He answered: "It is yet to come." For a man who once played professional football, was instrumental in creating the first Spanish-language TV network in the United States, and is a respected television newsman, broadcast executive, and leader in the Mexican-American community, that experience truly will have to be memorable. For Danny Villanueva has already experienced a lot.

Born in a mud hut in Tucumcari, New Mexico, in 1937, one of eleven children, the man who would later help win his station the valued National Peabody Award was classed as a "slow learner" in school.

That peculiar classification notwithstanding, young Danny made it through school just fine, then went on to receive his Bachelor of Arts degree from New Mexico State College, after which he turned to professional football.

He was a field-goal specialist, first with the Los Angeles Rams and then with the Dallas Cowboys. But while he loved sports, Villanueva felt that he could not serve the needs of his people playing football. He retired in 1968 and joined KMEX-TV, a Spanish-language station, as news director and as director of community relations. Two years later he was appointed vice-president and general manager.

He became what the *Los Angeles Times* calls "the self-appointed ombudsman for the entire Mexican-American community." An exponent of advocacy journalism, Villanueva involved himself deeply in the affairs of southern

California's large Spanish-speaking population and became a trusted spokesman for, and a welcome participant in, the activities of a large minority.

But that wasn't enough. For years Villanueva dreamed of a Spanish-language television network expanding beyond the borders of Los Angeles. In 1972 he saw the dream come true. SIN-West (SIN is for Spanish International Network), the first of its kind in the United States, was created.

With Danny doubling as vice-president and general manager of SIN-West while retaining the same position with KMEX-TV, the network serves three and a half million viewers in California and another million in Mexico. Spanish International Communications Corporation also owns stations in Miami, New York, Hanford-Fresno, and San Antonio, and has plans for further expansion.

At its inception, skeptics gave KMEX-TV six months to live. That was in 1962. Shortly thereafter, its news programming won a Peabody Award, the Pulitzer Prize for broadcast journalism, and today it heads a regional network.

"We're a cross between an educational and a commercial station," Villanueva explains. "We have a tremendous social obligation. The Spanish-speaking people don't have a *Time* or a *Newsweek*. So we leave the news to do social service. If we don't, nobody will."

Almost all of his free time is spent working for the Mexican-American community. When Danny isn't on the air or in his office, he is involved in speaking schedules, scholarship funds, and youth programs. He is also chairman of the board of a savings-and-loan company and former chairman of the California State Park and Recreation Commission.

His efforts on behalf of Mexican-Americans were recognized in 1971 when the Mexican-American Opportunity Foundation presented him with an Aztec Award for distinguished achievement toward development of opportunity for Mexican-American workers.

Asked in the same questionnaire that probed his most memorable experience who had had the most impact on his life, Villanueva replied, "My father. Because of his total dedication to serving others, his total commitment to his mission."

Like father, like son.

Carlos Villarreal

Carlos Villarreal

It's a long road from pumping gasoline to winning a presidential appointment on the Postal Rate Commission, and it takes a special kind of man to travel the distance. Such a man is Carlos Villarreal.

A child of poverty and sadness, Villarreal walked the long road to his first federal assignment in 1969 when he became steward of the one-billion-dollar Urban Mass Transportation Administration. He was one of Richard Nixon's highest-ranking Spanish-surnamed appointees.

Four years later he became one of five commissioners on the independent Postal Rate Commission, one of the nation's newest and most interesting federal regulatory agencies.

Villarreal was born in Brownsville, Texas, in 1924, and his mother died four years later. Young Carlos was raised by two maiden aunts, and by the time he was nine he was helping a depression-burdened family by working in a gas station.

He worked his way through high school and through classes at Texas A&M University before joining the Army. It was while in the service that Villarreal won a competitive examination for appointment in the U.S. Naval Academy. He was graduated from Annapolis in 1948.

Villarreal was the first member of his class to command a ship, and before his tour of duty during the Korean War was over, he had five ships under his operational command. High-ranking naval officials predicted that Villarreal would be an admiral someday, but he had other goals in mind.

Resigning from the Navy, he spent the next thirteen years advancing just as rapidly in the business world, beginning with the General Electric Company and then moving to the Marquardt Company as vice-president of marketing and administration.

It was as he was serving with Marquardt that Villarreal was appointed administrator for the Department of Transportation's Urban Mass Transportation Administration, a challenge he welcomed with concern for others: "The elderly, the handicapped, the poor, the very young, and the unemployed have not only an urgent need for, but also a basic right to, mobility."

President Nixon commended Villarreal for his leadership in spearheading the growth of the urban mass-transportation program from a $150-million item in the federal budget to a $1-billion undertaking.

Most of the money was for improving bus, rapid-transit, and commuter service throughout the nation. Villarreal completely restructured the research-and-development program to emphasize new services and equipment.

After four years as administrator of the UMTA, he was anxious to retire from public life, but President Nixon persuaded Villarreal to accept yet another job, and in 1973 appointed him to the Postal Rate Commission.

As one of five commissioners responsible for determining postal rates and mail classifications, Villarreal finds himself dealing with a service which affects all levels of society through the transmittal of ninety billion pieces of mail.

It adds up to a ten-billion-dollar-a-year business. Postal-rate cases before the commission comprise the largest utility-type rate proceedings in the nation.

When Mrs. Anne Armstrong, counselor to the President, administered the oath of office to Villarreal, she said: "It is easy to see that Carlos Villarreal is a man of many talents. As Administrator of the UMTA, he qualified for and received a bus operator's license. And I understand he now is in the latter stages of getting his private pilot's license. If he runs true to form, he probably will be involved in delivering the mail just to prove he can do it."

In his own message to others of Mexican-American heritage, Villarreal called on them to take pride in their heritage and in their country. "I am a patriot," he said. "I love my country. I am an American first and a Spanish-surnamed citizen second."

He has demonstrated with accomplishment and concern that it is not only possible but also imperative to be immensely proud of both.

Other MENTOR Books of Special Interest

☐ **PAIN AND PROMISE: THE CHICANO TODAY edited and with an Introduction by Edward Simmen.** Thirty-two essays on the dramatic emergence of the Mexican-American from passive endurance of century-old indifference and injustice at the hands of Anglo society. Included are essays by César Chávez, José Angel Gutíerrez, Reies Lopez Tijerina and Philip D. Ortego.

(#MY1139—$1.25)

☐ **THE CHICANO: FROM CARICATURE TO SELF-PORTRAIT edited and with an Introduction by Edward Simmen.** An anthology of short stories offering for the first time a collection of writings devoted exclusively to the Mexican American. These stories, often comic, sometimes tragic —present the Mexican American as an individual caught in a social order that demands he meet that society on its own terms—or suffer.

(#MW1069—$1.50)

☐ **BLACK VOICES: An Anthology of Afro-American Literature edited by Abraham Chapman.** An exciting and varied anthology of fiction, autobiography, poetry, and literary criticism by America's Black writers, among them Ralph Ellison, Richard Wright, and James Baldwin.

(#ME1265—$1 ⁵)

☐ **BLACK VIEWPOINTS edited by Arthur C. Littleton and Mary W. Burger.** The more than fifty essays in this thought-provoking anthology deal almost exclusively with the Black man of the twentieth century—his aspirations, frustrations and his image of himself. The writers include Malcolm X, Dick Gregory, Eldridge Cleaver, Shirley Chisholm, and others. (#MY1079—$1.50)

More MENTOR Books of Special Interest

☐ **THE NEGRO IN AMERICAN CULTURE by Margaret Just Butcher.** A unique creative work which places the contributions of Black Americans firmly within the framework of the nation's creative thought. Ms. Butcher explores the Black's role in music, the theater, art, literature, education and politics. (#MW1345—$1.50)

☐ **THE BLACK WOMAN: An Anthology edited by Toni Cade.** What is the reality of being Black, being a woman, and living in America—a society that still regards the Black woman as "the slave's slave"? With this collection we at last hear her voice expressing her opinions on such subjects as politics, racism, the Black man, Black pride and many other topics. Included are Abbey Lincoln, Joanne Grant, Nikki Giovanni and Kay Lindsey.
(#MY1311—$1.25)

☐ **NEW BLACK VOICES: An Anthology of Contemporary Afro-American Literature edited and with an Introduction by Abraham Chapman.** An unprecedented anthology of the contributions of Black Americans in the fields of poetry, fiction, literary criticism and documents. Included are **James Baldwin** and **Eldridge Cleaver.**
(#MW1116—$1.50)

☐ **BEYOND THE ANGRY BLACK edited by John A. Williams.** In this gripping collection of stories, articles and poems, some of America's best known authors—black and white—answer the unasked questions raised by the lack of racial communication in all phases of life. Included are Langston Hughes, Chester Himes and Carrie Allen Young. (#MY1058—$1.25)

THE NEW AMERICAN LIBRARY, INC.,
P.O. Box 999, Bergenfield, New Jersey 07621

Please send me the MENTOR BOOKS I have checked above. I am enclosing $_____(check or money order—no currency or C.O.D.'s). Please include the list price plus 25¢ a copy to cover handling and mailing costs. (Prices and numbers are subject to change without notice.)

9519124

Name_____

Address_____

City_____ State_____ Zip Code_____
Allow at least 3 weeks for delivery